KU-323-762

Asymptomatic Coronary Artery Disease & Angina

MEDICAL LIBRARY
WATFORD POSTGRADUATE
MEDICAL CENTRE
WATFORD GENERAL HOSPITAL
VICARAGE ROAD
WATFORD WD1 8HB

Asymptomatic Coronary Artery Disease & Angina

Edited by
John Cleland
British Heart Foundation Fellow
MRC Clinical Research
Initiative in Heart Failure
University of Glasgow
Glasgow, UK

With contributions from
David Wood
National Heart & Lung Institute
London, UK

Gordon Lowe
Department of Medicine
Glasgow Royal Infirmary
Glasgow, UK

Iain Findlay and Luciano Moretti
Department of Cardiology
Royal Alexandra Hospital
Paisley, UK

John McMurray
Department of Cardiology
Western Infirmary
Glasgow, UK

Presented as a service
to medicine by

SCIENCE PRESS

© Copyright 1996 by Science Press Ltd, 34–42 Cleveland St, London, W1P 6LB, UK.

All rights reserved. No part of this publication may be reproduced, stored in a retrieval system or transmitted in any form or by any means electronic, mechanical, photo-copying, recording or otherwise without prior permission of the publishers.

British Library Cataloguing in Publication Data

A catalogue record for this book is available from the British Library

ISBN 1-85873-076-7

This copy of *Asymptomatic Coronary Artery Disease and Angina* is given as a service to medicine by Bayer plc. Sponsorship of this copy does not imply the sponsor's agree-ment or otherwise with the views expressed herein.

Although every effort has been made to ensure that drug doses and other information are presented accurately in this publication, the ultimate responsibility rests with the prescribing physician. Neither the publishers nor the authors can be held responsible for errors or for any consequences arising from the use of the information contained herein. Any product mentioned in this publication should be used in accordance with the prescribing information prepared by the manufacturers. No claims or endorse-ments are made for any drug or compound at present under clinical investigation.

Project editor: Hilary Dean
Illustrator: Matthew McCutcheon
Typesetters: Paul Angliss and Simon Banister
Cover design: Claire Huntley
Production: Kate Oldfield
Indexer: Anne McCarthy
Printed in Italy

10 9 8 7 6 5 4 3 2 1

Contents

Clinical epidemiology
David Wood

The frequency and prognosis of coronary disease, which includes stable angina, unstable angina and acute myocardial infarction (MI), can be reliably described only from studies of the general population. Selected hospital cases give a biased picture of the disease's clinical characteristics, course and prognosis. A contemporary description of the development of symptomatic coronary heart disease (CHD) in the community is provided by the Hillingdon CHD Register [1], which, unlike earlier surveys [2–4], included new (incident) cases of stable and unstable angina, in addition to acute MI and sudden cardiac death.

The Hillingdon CHD Register

This register was set up at the Hillingdon Hospital in London, UK, in 1993 to identify incident cases of coronary disease in a population of 159 600 patients served by 80 general practitioners. All new cases of angina were referred to a rapid-access chest pain clinic at the hospital. Eligible patients were those presenting for the first time with chest pain but with no prior medical history of CHD, who were considered by the general practitioner to have stable angina. Those patients thought to have acute ischaemia (unstable angina) or MI were admitted directly to hospital in the usual way. Surveillance of the accident and emergency department, cardiac care unit and general medical wards identified these patients. Finally, all sudden cardiac deaths in previously healthy individuals in the practice population attributed to coronary artery disease at postmortem examination were identified by the coroner. The incidence of all major clinical manifestations of CHD was recorded prospectively and is shown in Figure 1.1.

Fig. 1.1. Incidence of first presentations of coronary heart disease in the Hillingdon CHD Register (n = 192). Angina (both stable and unstable) accounted for 44% of all symptomatic manifestations of CHD in this population, and most of these patients were considered stable at the point of presentation.

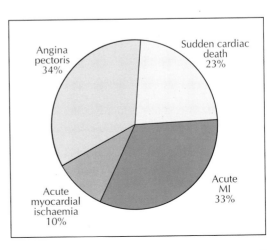

Angina pectoris 34%

Sudden cardiac death 23%

Acute MI 33%

Acute myocardial ischaemia 10%

Population surveys of incidence and prognosis of stable angina

Incidence of stable angina

Five prospective studies of incident angina have been reported [5–9]. More prevalence studies than prospective studies have been carried out but, as in the British Regional Heart Study [10], they simply estimate disease burden at one point in time. Thus they provide much less information than prospective surveys, which measure both incidence and outcome.

The characteristics of the five prospective studies are shown in Figure 1.2. With the exception of the Southampton survey [9], all studies were reported in the 1970s, before the widespread use of revascularization by coronary bypass surgery and more recently by angioplasty. The Southampton survey, conducted in 1990, was based on a chest pain clinic set up at the Royal South Hants Hospital that offered an open-access service to a random sample of 117 general practices serving an adult population of 192 000 patients. As for the Hillingdon CHD register, general practitioners agreed to refer all new patients aged less than 70 years presenting for the first time with chest pain that could be due to CHD. Patients with a prior medical history of CHD were excluded.

Patients were assessed by a cardiology registrar within 24 h of seeing their general practitioner. After a full history and physical examination, resting electrocardiogram (ECG) and chest radiography, the patient was classified as having definite angina on the basis of the following criteria:

- recurrent attacks of brief (up to 15 min) episodes of chest pain, precipitated by exertion, or exertion and emotion, relieved by rest; character and radiation of chest pain consistent with the diagnosis.

When some (but not all) characteristics were present, the patient was classified as having 'possible angina'.

A total of 467 patients were referred, of whom 110 (24%) had definite angina (70 men, 40 women) and 63 (13%) possible angina (39 men, 24 women). The complete diagnostic classification of the remaining patients is shown in Figure 1.3. The clinical characteristics of patients with definite angina are shown in Figure 1.4. Resting ECG showed 1 mm downsloping ST-segment depression in 5% of patients with definite angina and in none of the patients with possible angina, Q/QS patterns in 4% of patients with angina and in none of those with possible angina, complete left bundle branch block in one patient with definite and one with possible angina, and right bundle branch block in one with definite and two with possible angina. In patients with definite or possible angina who underwent exercise testing, ECG ischaemia (≥ 1 mm ST-segment depression) was provoked in 61% and 32%, respectively. In the definite angina group, 29% (30/103) had marked ischaemia (≥ 3 mm downsloping ST-segment depression) on exercise testing.

The referral rate was 192 patients per 100 000 per annum in a patient population aged less than 70 years (Fig. 1.5).

2

Study	Population	Diagnosis and investigations	Incidence (number/1000/year)	Prognosis
Framingham Study 1972 [5]	Healthy Interviewed at examinations every 2 years 30–62 years	Clinical, by 3 physicians (structured questionnaire) ECG and CXR	3% (< 1%) in 40–44-year-olds, 11%M and 8%W in 60–64-year-olds.	At 14 years, 48%M and 25%W had other manifestations of CHD (MI/death), of whom 58% (52%) died Remission occurred in 32%M and 44%W for at least 2 years.
Israeli Ischaemic Heart Disease 1976 [6,11]	Healthy male civil service employees < 40 years	Clinical, by a number of physicians (structured questionnaire) ECG	New angina: 5.7 (age-adjusted)	At 5 years, 85% were well, 7% suffered an MI, 3% died and 5% were unreported.
Fry 1976 [7]	Healthy 1 general practice population of 2755 adults > 40 years	Clinical, by 1 GP	5 (23% angina with MI)	At 20 years, 50% of patients died, 75% of these from cardiovascular causes 7% developed complications (MI and heart failure). The angina persisted in 25% and resolved in 18%
Duncan 1976 [8]	Men with chest pain, referred from 71 GPs with 28 400 men 35–69 years	Clinical, by 1 cardiologist ECG, CXR, enzymes, with exercise test if diagnosis doubtful	1.8 (10% had a history of MI)	At 6 months, 14% had developed complications (MI and death)
Gandhi 1995 [9]	Patients with new chest pain, referred from 117 GPs with a population of 191 677 < 70 years	Clinical, by 1 cardiologist (structured questionnaire) ECG, CXR, exercise test and 24-h ambulatory ECG tape	0.83 (95% CI 0.66, 1.0)	At 15.8 months (range 7–30), 11% of patients developed MI or died and 19% underwent revascularization.

Fig. 1.2. Incidence and prognosis of angina pectoris in population surveys. CI, confidence intervals; CXR, chest radiology; GP, general practitioner; M, men; W, women.

3

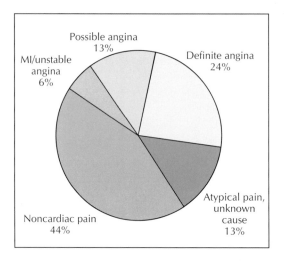

Fig. 1.3. Clinical classification of chest pain referrals to the Southampton chest pain clinic (n = 467).

Clinical characteristic	Number
Mean age, years	57.4 (SD 9.6)
Male:female ratio	70:40 (64:36%)

Smoking habit
    current smoker
    ex-smoker
    pipe or cigar smoker
    life-long nonsmoker
	
	33 (30%)
	47 (43%)
	5 (4%)
	25 (23%)

Body mass index, kg/m²
    < 25
    25–29
    ≥ 30
	
	24 (22%)
	55 (50%)
	30 (28%)

Hypertension*	53 (48%)

Cholesterol, mmol/l
    < 6.5
    6.5–7.9
    ≥ 8.0
	
	26 (25%)
	49 (47%)
	29 (28%)

Diabetes mellitus†	9 (9%)

Resting ECG
    ≥ 1 mm STD
    Q/QS‡
    LBBB
	
	5 (5%)
	5 (4%)
	1 (1%)

Exercise ECG
    ≥ 1 mm STD
    ≥ 3 mm STD
	
	63 (61%)
	30 (29%)

Fig. 1.4. Clinical characteristics of 110 patients presenting with angina pectoris from a randomly selected general population sample. *Blood pressure ≥160/100mmHg or on antihypertensive medication; †random glucose >11 mmol/l or on medication; ‡Minnesota code 1.1, 1.2. LBBB, left bundle branch block; SD, standard deviation; STD, horizontal or downsloping ST-segment depression. Adapted with permission from Gandhi et al. [9].

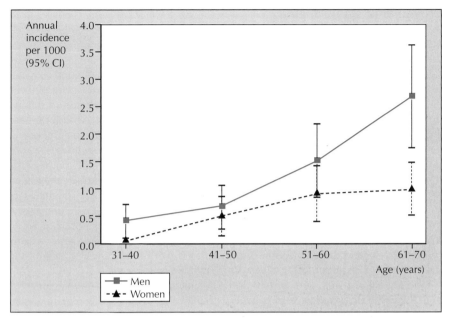

Fig. 1.5. *Age- and sex-specific incidence of definite angina shows a rise in incidence with age in both men and women, with twice as many cases in the oldest age group of 61–70 years. CI, confidence interval.*

The incidence of angina in the Southampton survey is lower than in the four previous studies [5–8]. Incidence rates in men range from 0.59 to 5.7 per 1000 per annum, a nine-fold difference between studies. This may reflect real variation in CHD incidence between the different populations but changes in incidence over time between the Southampton study and the earlier studies must also be taken into account. Contemporary angina incidence rates are likely to be substantially lower in the Southampton study than those recorded in the Framingham study, given the real decline in incidence and mortality of other acute manifestations of CHD. Methodological differences between these studies could also contribute to the variation in rates. Differences in the age and sex structure of the study populations, diagnostic criteria for angina (whether other manifestations of CHD were included) and statistical confidence in calculations could all contribute to the observed variation.

When the Southampton angina incidence rates are applied to the UK population of approximately 60 million, assuming that disease frequency is the same throughout the country, 22 000 new angina cases in patients aged less than 70 years might be expected annually. This is probably an underestimate because the incidence of angina in the South of England is likely to be lower than in other parts of the UK because CHD mortality rises towards the North and West. More than 17 000 of these new angina patients will have ischaemia on exercise testing, 29% with sufficient evidence of severe ischaemia to consider coronary angiography at the point of presentation.

Prognosis of stable angina

Investigators in all five prospective studies [5–9,11] have reported prognosis (see Fig. 1.2) but the values for morbidity and mortality are not directly comparable, given the developments in managing angina in the past 30 years. In the Framingham study [12], half of the men and one-quarter of the women with angina had another manifestation of CHD (MI or death or both) in 14 years of follow-up and about half of these events were deaths [5]. In the Southampton study [9] the median duration of follow-up was only 15.8 months (range 7–30 months) and, although almost one-fifth of these patients were revascularized by balloon angioplasty or coronary artery surgery, one in ten still progressed to MI (n=8) or coronary death (n=4). Event-free survival is shown in Figure 1.6. Most of these deaths and MIs occurred early in the clinical course of the disease, so, if interventions are to reduce morbidity and mortality further, they need to be performed sooner than is current practice in the UK. As in the Framingham study, in which remission of angina for at least 2 years in one-third of men and almost half of women was reported, the Southampton study investigators observed spontaneous resolution of symptoms in about one in ten patients in the short term. Angina is a clinical syndrome and therefore whether this is part of the clinical course of the disease or a consequence of misdiagnosis of symptoms is uncertain.

The SAPAT trial [13], although not an epidemiological study, had the largest long-term follow-up of a population of patients with mild angina not initially requiring intervention for the management of symptoms. The investigators compared aspirin and placebo in a population treated with background beta blocker therapy. More than 2000 patients were followed for a median of 50 months. Patients with a history of MI were excluded, so most of the study population could be assumed to have well preserved

| | Outcome | | Months to | |
	Male (n = 69)	Female (n = 38)	event (median)	Total events (%)
No. of patients who died	4	0	2.6	3.7
No. of patients who had MI	6	2	1.6	7.5
No. of patients who underwent PTCA*	9	3	2.9	11.2
No. of patients who underwent CABG†	8	0	7.5	7.5

Fig. 1.6. *Outcome of patients presenting with typical angina in the general population. *Excluding one female patient on waiting list; †excluding one female and two male patients on waiting list; CABG, coronary artery bypass grafting; PTCA, percutaneous transluminal coronary angioplasty.*

ventricular function. Among the 1009 patients taking aspirin and beta blocker, only 47 nonfatal infarcts occurred (about 1 infarct per 100 patients/year). During the 50-month follow-up, 82 deaths occurred (about 2% per annum) but only 34 of these were cardiac in origin and could have been influenced by revascularization. The study population probably consisted of low-risk patients relatively free of pulmonary and peripheral vascular disease, in view of the requirement for beta blocker use, and other complicating conditions.

Population surveys of incidence and prognosis of unstable angina

Patients with acute myocardial ischaemia (unstable angina) but without evidence of infarction accounted for 10% of all clinical manifestations of coronary disease in the Hillingdon CHD Register [1]. Only one prospective population study of new and worsening angina has been reported [8]. This included patients whose symptoms increased in frequency or severity without objective evidence of definite recent MI. The study was conducted in the 1970s in a special clinic at the Royal Infirmary of Edinburgh over 2.5 years, covering a population of 28 400 men (35–69 years) served by 71 general practitioners. All men under 70 years of age were referred who had experienced chest pain suggestive of myocardial ischaemia during the previous 4 weeks either occurring for the first time (new cases), recurring after an interval of freedom of 1 month (recurrent) or abruptly and unexpectedly increasing in frequency and severity (exacerbations) in the absence of a myocardial infarct.

A total of 251 patients fulfilled the criteria for new or worsening angina, 21 of whom had possible MI with prolonged pain or equivocal ECG changes at their first visit. Of the 251 patients, 129 presented with angina for the first time (10% had previous MI and 103 presented with exacerbations). The incidence of serious cardiac complications (sudden death, definite or probable MI or resuscitated collapse) was 15.5% for the whole population over 6 months and the complication rates did not differ between groups, with a rate of 16.5% in those with exacerbations of angina. Of the 39 patients who suffered complications, 28 (72%) did so within 6 months and most of these events occurred within 12 weeks of the onset of symptoms. Of these serious cardiac complications, 9 (4%) were deaths and 30 (12%) patients developed MI but survived. In the group of patients who survived without developing MI, 66 (31%) had no angina at 6 months.

Clinical selection of patients for inhospital investigation and treatment, compared with treatment in general practice, was no better than the play of chance in terms of subsequent prognosis. Of the 87 patients admitted to hospital because of prolonged chest pain or progressive worsening angina, 10 (11.5%) had serious cardiac complications up to 6 months after their initial referral to the clinic. This complication rate did not differ significantly from the 23 (14%) who had serious cardiac complications but were not admitted during the same period. As for the Framingham study, the Edinburgh study was based on clinical history and resting ECG only. Exercise tests were performed only where the diagnosis was in doubt and no routine coronary angiography was undertaken.

Study	[14]	[15]	[16]	[17,18]	[19]
Characteristics					
Population	Occ	Occ	Vol	Occ	Occ
No. of patients	1390	(325)*	108	2014	4842
Age, years					
range	20–54	20–54	40–64	40–59	40–59
mean	38	43	46	50	49
Prevalence of asymptomatic ischaemia (%)					
Ex. test/Holter	10 (140)	(111)*	15 (16)	3.7 (75)	9.1 (439)
Noninvasive imaging	ND	ND	34 (37)	ND	ND
Both	ND	ND	12 (13)	ND	2.4 (104)
Angiography (on +ve screening)	ND	3.1 (34)†	12 (13)	2.5 (50)	0.9 (25)‡
Subsequent clinical coronary disease					
Measured?	Yes	ND	Yes	Yes	ND
Follow-up	6.4 years	NA	3 years	15 years	NA
% with asymptomatic ischaemia	20 (28/140)	NA	23 (3/13)	66 (33/50)	NA
% without asymptomatic ischaemia	1.4 (18/250)	NA	2 (2/95)	ND	NA

Fig. 1.7. *Prevalence of asymptomatic ischaemia in apparently healthy male volunteers in studies using coronary angiography. Number of events or patients in brackets. Coronary angiography was performed only on those with positive noninvasive screening test results, thus percentages assume no false-negative screening tests. *The second USAF study has no clear denominator; † angiography percentage (3.1%) assumes same prevalence of positive screening tests as for initial USAF study; ‡ in ECCIS, 387 (88%) of the 439 with positive exercise tests or Holter monitoring had noninvasive imaging and 62 (60%) of the 104 with positive noninvasive imaging tests had coronary angiography; percentages are adjusted for those drop outs; Ex. test, exercise test; NA, not applicable; ND, no data; Occ, occupational cohort; Vol, volunteers. Adapted with permission from Bowker [27].*

Frequency and prognosis of asymptomatic CHD

The frequency (prevalence) of asymptomatic myocardial ischaemia in apparently healthy individuals has been investigated in several studies, both with [14–19] and without [20–26] coronary angiography.

Noninvasive evidence of asymptomatic myocardial ischaemia is determined in various ways, including ST-segment changes on exercise testing or Holter monitoring, thallium perfusion abnormalities on exercise or with pharmacological stress and echocardio-graphic or radionuclide ventriculography. All these tests require a 'gold standard' for

Study	[20]	[21]	[22]	[23]	[24]	[25]	[26]
Characteristics							
Population	Vol	Occ	Vol	Occ	Com	Vol	Com
No. of patients	50	10 723	80	916	111	407	95
Sex	Male	Both	Both	Male	Both	Both	Both
Age, years							
range	35–59	18–65	20–50	27–55	20–67	40–96	35–71
mean	45	45	4 strata of 20	37	41	60	56
Prevalence of asymptomatic ischaemia (%)							
Ex. test/Holter	30 (15)	1.3 (135)	2.5 (2)	2.5 (23)	15.3 (17)	16 (66)	9.5 (9)
Noninvasive imaging	ND	ND	ND	ND	ND	14 (55)	ND
Both	ND	ND	ND	ND	10.9 (5/7)	6 (23)	ND
Subsequent clinical coronary disease							
Measured?	ND	Yes	ND	Yes	ND	Yes	ND
Follow-up	NA	6 years	NA	13 years	NA	4.6 years	NA
% with asymptomatic ischaemia	NA	15.6 (21/135)	NA	39 (9/23)	NA	48 (11/23)	NA
% without asymptomatic ischaemia	NA	3.4* (13/379)	NA	5.3 (44/833)	NA	7 (23/309)	NA

Fig. 1.8. *Prevalence of asymptomatic ischaemia in apparently healthy volunteers in studies not using coronary angiography. Number of events or patients in brackets. *The Milan study had 379 'controls' with negative screening test results as the comparison group; Com, community; Ex. test, exercise test; NA, not applicable; ND, no data; Occ, occupational cohort; Vol, volunteers. Adapted with permission from Bowker [27].*

myocardial ischaemia and, although angiographic coronary artery disease is the usual standard against which such tests are compared, this is not synonymous with ischaemia. Furthermore, such an invasive investigation cannot, for ethical reasons, be performed in all healthy people and is necessarily restricted to those who show evidence of myocardial ischaemia from other tests. The prevalence of coronary artery disease in those with no evidence of myocardial ischaemia on noninvasive testing is, therefore, not known. An alternative 'gold standard' is the subsequent clinical outcome of those screened and, unlike the need for selection in coronary angiography, every healthy person can be followed up for morbidity and mortality. Studies using coronary angiography on apparently healthy individuals are described in Figure 1.7 and those not using this standard in Figure 1.8.

Asymptomatic coronary disease detected in apparently healthy people is estimated at 9.1–15.3% in the general population and this is associated with a significantly increased risk of developing symptomatic coronary disease. No randomized controlled trial evidence exists to indicate whether intervention (medical or surgical) in those with asymptomatic disease reduces the risk of subsequent morbidity and mortality. Until such evidence becomes available, screening the healthy population to detect asymptomatic myocardial ischaemia is not justified.

Characteristics of patients with angina in primary care

The studies discussed so far have concentrated on the clinical characteristics of patients with new-onset angina but prevalent cases (survivors) also need to be considered. The largest cross-sectional study of patients with angina was reported recently in a US population drawn from primary care [28]. Although this was a large sample, it may have been biased towards older low-risk patients because they were being cared for by the primary care physicians. Despite this, the population is probably more representative of most patients with angina than hospital-based series. More than half of the study population were women, with an average age of 69 years. Patient characteristics are given in Figures 1.9 and 1.10. In contrast to the majority of patients recruited into studies of angina, most patients had more than one additional disease. Overall, 25% of

	Age group (years)			
	< 60 (n = 1006)	60–69 (n = 1434)	70–79 (n = 1582)	> 79 (n = 914)
Systemic hypertension*	55	60	59	55
MI	39	41	45	53
Hypercholesterolaemia†	39	39	33	21
Congestive heart failure	14	19	28	42
Diabetes mellitus	23	26	23	19
Arrhythmia	14	18	25	30
PTCA/CABG	15	16	12	5
Conduction disturbance	4	4	7	8
No associated illness	9	6	6	4
> 1 associated illness	64	69	72	74

Fig. 1.9. *Patient characteristics in the largest cross-sectional study of angina in primary-care: cardiovascular-associated illnesses. *Systolic blood pressure > 169 mmHg or diastolic blood pressure > 90 mmHg; †total cholesterol > 260 mg/dl or low-density lipoprotein cholesterol > 190 mg/dl, or the ratio of total cholesterol to high-density lipoprotein cholesterol > 5.0; CABG, coronary artery bypass grafting; PTCA, percutaneous transluminal coronary angioplasty. Adapted with permission from Pepine et al. [28].*

	Age group (years)			
	<60 (n = 1006)	60–69 (n = 1434)	70–79 (n = 1582)	>79 (n = 914)
Calcium antagonists	47	49	45	44
Nitrates	57	63	62	62
Beta blockers	27	27	25	19
Diuretics/other antihypertensives	28	33	40	43
Potassium supplements	11	16	21	22
Digoxin	8	15	22	27
ACE inhibitors	13	16	14	14
No cardiovascular drugs	11	9	7	7
>1 cardiovascular drug	57	65	67	69

Fig. 1.10. *Patient characteristics in the largest cross-sectional study of angina in primary care: prevalence (%) of cardiovascular medical therapies. ACE, angiotensin converting enzyme. Adapted with permission from Pepine et al. [28].*

the study population had heart failure, 23% diabetes and 58% hypertension. Although 90% of patients had exertional angina, 47% also had episodes of angina at rest and 35% had chest pain evoked by mental stress.

Summary

Distinguishing from symptoms alone between clinical syndromes can be difficult and selection of patients for referral to hospital, either acutely or to outpatients, is inevitably imprecise. As a consequence, patients with stable myocardial ischaemia or even non-cardiac pain are admitted to cardiac care units and conversely patients with acute ischaemia or an evolving MI can be inadvertently looked after in the community.

At first presentation with chest pain that is suspicious of myocardial ischaemia, a specialist opinion and investigation is required in all cases. This is conveniently provided through a daily rapid-access chest pain service located in a district general hospital. Such a service will clarify the diagnosis and, through appropriate investigations, identify those patients who may benefit from revascularization.

Progression to MI or coronary death in patients with angina (stable and unstable) occurs in 11–16.5% of such patients in the short term and most of these events actually occur in the first few weeks or months after medical diagnosis.

Whether early revascularization in this setting will modify the prognosis of angina has yet to be determined in a randomized controlled trial. Interventions aimed at reducing the risk of MI and coronary death, such as coronary revascularization, will be required much earlier in the clinical course of the disease than is currently the case if these interventions are to improve prognosis.

References

1. Roberts RH et al.: The incidence and presentation of ischaemic heart disease: a population survey [Abstract]. Br Heart J 1995, 73(suppl 3):49.
2. Armstrong A et al.: Natural history of acute coronary heart attacks. Br Heart J 1972, 34:67–80.
3. Kinlen LJ: Incidence and presentation of myocardial infarction in an English community. Br Heart J 1973, 35:616–622.
4. Tunstall-Pedoe H et al.: Coronary heart attacks in East London. Lancet 1975, ii:833–838.
5. Kannel W, Feinleib M: Natural history of angina pectoris in the Framingham Study. Am J Cardiol 1972, 29:154–163.
6. Medalie JH et al.: Angina pectoris among 10,000 men. 5 year incidence and univariate analysis. Am J Med 1973, 55:583–594.
7. Fry J: The natural history of angina in a general practice. J R Coll Gen Pract 1976, 26:643–646.
8. Duncan B et al.: Prognosis of new and worsening angina pectoris. BMJ 1976, 1:981–985.
9. Gandhi MM et al.: Incidence, clinical characteristics and short-term prognosis of angina pectoris. Br Heart J 1995, 73:193–198.
10. Shaper A et al.: Prevalence of ischaemic heart disease in middle aged British men. Br Heart J 1984, 51:595–605.
11. Medalie JH, Goldbourt U: Angina pectoris among 10,000 men. II. Psychosocial and other risk factors as evidenced by a multivariate analysis of a five incidence study. Am J Med 1976, 60:910–921.
12. Kannell WB, Sorlie PD: Remission of clinical angina pectoris: the Framingham Study. Am J Cardiol 1978, 42:119–123.
13. Jull Moller S et al.: Double-blind trial of aspirin in primary prevention of myocardial infarction in patients with stable angina pectoris. Lancet 1992, 340:1421–1425.
14. Froelicher VF et al.: Epidemiologic study of asymptomatic men screened by maximal treadmill testing for latent coronary artery disease. Am J Cardiol 1974, 34:770–776.
15. Froelicher VF et al.: Angiographic findings in asymptomatic aircrewmen with electrocardiographic abnormalities. Am J Cardiol 1977, 39:32–38.
16. Langou RA et al.: Predicitve accuracy of coronary artery calcification and abnormal exercise test for coronary artery disease in asymptomatic men. Circulation 1980, 62:1196–1203.
17. Erikssen J et al.: False positive diagnostic tests and coronary angiographic findings in 105 presumably healthy males. Circulation 1976, 54:371–376.
18. Thaulow E et al.: Initial clinical presentation of cardiac disease in asymptomatic men with silent myocardial ischaemia and angiographically documented coronary artery diseae (the Oslo ischaemia study). Am J Cardiol 1993, 72:629–633.
19. Fazzini PF et al.: Epidemiology of silent myocardial ischaemia in asymptomatic middle-aged men (the ECCIS project). Am J Cardiol 1993, 72:1383–1388.
20. Armstrong WF et al.: Prevalence and magnitude of ST segment and T wave abnormalities in normal men during continuous ambulatory electrocardiography. Am J Cardiol 1982, 49: 1638–1642.
21. Giagoni E et al.: Prognostic value of exercise ECG testing in asymptomatic normotensive subjects. N Engl J Med 1983, 309:1085–1089.
22. Deanfield JE et al.: Analysis of ST segment changes in normal subjects: implications for ambulatory monitoring in angina pectoris. Am J Cardiol 1984, 54:1321–1325.
23. McHenry PL et al.: The abnormal exercise electrocardiogram in apparently healthy men: a predictor of angina pectoris as an initial coronary event during long-term follow-up. Circulation 1984, 70: 547–551.
24. Kohli RS et al.: The segment of the ambulatory electrocardiogram in a normal population. Br Heart J 1988, 60:4–16.
25. Fleg JL et al.: Prevalence and prognosic significance of exercise induced silent myocardial ischaemia detected by thallium scintigraphy and electrocardiography in asymptomatic volunteers. Circulation 1990, 81:428–436.
26. Gandhi MM et al.: Characteristics and clinical significance of ambulatory myocardial ischaemia in men and women in the general population presenting with angina pectoris. J Am Coll Cardiol 1994, 23:74–81.
27. Bowker TJ: Covert coronary disease and non-invasive evidence of covert myocardial ischaemia: their prevalence and implications [Editorial]. Int J Cardiol 1994, 45:1–7.
27. Pepine CJ et al.: Characteristics of a contemporary population with angina pectoris. Am J Cardiol 1994, 74:226–231.

Risk factors in cardiovascular disease
Gordon Lowe

Introduction

Traditionally, interest in risk factors for cardiovascular disease has focused on their assessment and modification in 'healthy' persons without clinical evidence of arterial disease. This resulted from the belief that risk factor modification would only be of value in reducing the risk of arterial disease and its major complications — coronary death, MI, angina, ischaemic strokes, transient cerebral ischaemic attacks, claudication and critical limb ischaemia — before their onset.

In recent years, enthusiasm for primary prevention of cardiovascular events in the healthy population has waned for several reasons.

- The classic, potentially reversible risk factors (smoking, cholesterol, blood pressure, obesity) have been discovered to be rather inefficient predictors of high cardiovascular risk [1,2].

- In randomized trials of cholesterol-lowering, benefit was most obvious in the 9% of the study population with a high initial risk of cardiovascular events, most of whom had experienced MI before trial entry [2]. Almost 50% of the study populations in these trials were at low initial risk of cardiovascular events and fared no better on therapy. This may be related to the inverse associations of cholesterol with cancer and with haemorrhagic stroke [3,4].

- In randomized trials of blood pressure reduction, a relatively small reduction was seen in ischaemic heart disease events (14%), although a larger reduction was seen in stroke risk (42%) [5].

- Little benefit was seen in randomized trials of multiple risk factor interventions, such as the MRFIT study [6].

- Motivating asymptomatic people and their families to change their lifestyles or take long-term medications (e.g. to lower cholesterol or blood pressure) is difficult.

- Primary prevention involves high cost–benefit and risk–benefit ratios for health services that are under increasing financial pressure.

At the same time, enthusiasm for secondary prevention of cardiovascular events in those with clinically evident cardiovascular disease has increased, again for various reasons.

- Investigators in several trials have demonstrated that regression of arterial stenoses in the femoral, coronary and carotid arteries can occur, for example during cholesterol reduction [7].

- Ischaemic events result not only from progressive atherosclerotic stenoses but also from other pathological processes, including rupture of arterial plaques (which are not necessarily stenotic), platelet-fibrin thrombosis, alterations in local vasoactive factors promoting arterial spasm and the rheological effects of blood viscosity factors that modify blood flow not only in the supplying artery but also in the ischaemic microcirculation [8–10]. The effects of risk factor reduction on these non-atherosclerotic processes may be relatively rapid compared with their long-term effects in reducing atherosclerotic progression [8].

- Patients with clinically evident arterial disease have a higher absolute risk (approximately one order of magnitude) of cardiovascular events compared with those without such evidence. If the relative benefits of risk factor modification are similar in both groups, then the absolute benefits will be several times higher in those at greater risk.

- Symptomatic patients and their families are more motivated to change their lifestyles and take long-term medications, compared with those who are asymptomatic.

- Secondary prevention has lower cost–benefit and risk–benefit ratios than primary prevention.

Most natural history and secondary prevention studies in patients with clinically evident arterial disease have been performed on those with ischaemic heart disease (e.g. angina, survivors of MI). However, recent epidemiological studies have confirmed that patients with peripheral or cerebral arterial disease have a profile of potentially reversible risk factors, as shown by Gordon *et al.* more than 20 years ago [11], and similar high risk of cardiovascular events [4,12]. Therefore, practising secondary prevention is as important in patients with clinically evident peripheral or cerebrovascular disease as in those with clinically evident ischaemic heart disease. Symptoms of peripheral disease, such as claudication and slow walking due to hemiparesis, may mask symptoms of angina. Angina would otherwise be common because many patients with peripheral arterial or cerebrovascular disease have coronary artery disease [4,12].

Risk factors and risk predictors

A cardiovascular risk predictor is a biological variable that has been shown in prospective studies to predict increased risk of cardiovascular events. Many risk predictors are not modifiable (e.g. age, sex, family history of premature cardiovascular disease) but may still be clinically useful in predicting absolute risk of cardiovascular events in an individual patient and, hence, in guiding clinical decisions for risk factor modification based on assessments of benefits and risks to the patient and costs to the practice and health service.

A cardiovascular risk factor is not only a risk predictor but also plays a biological role in promoting cardiovascular events. The classic criteria of Bradford Hill [13] for risk factor status of a variable include the strength of the association, its consistency, its dose-dependence, its presence before the onset of disease, the biological plausibility that it might promote disease, and finally the demonstration that reduction in exposure to the variable results in reduction of disease.

This chapter concentrates on risk factors for cardiovascular events, in particular death, MI and stroke, in patients with clinically evident arterial disease (angina, MI, stroke, transient ischaemic attacks, claudication, critical limb ischaemia) and in those who have undergone bypass grafting, angioplasty, endarterectomy or amputation because of such disease.

Age
The risk of cardiovascular events increases strongly with age irrespective of the presence of arterial disease. Although age is useful in assessing absolute risk of cardiovascular events, the impact of smoking [14] and cholesterol on relative cardiovascular risk is greater in younger adults.

Sex
Men have a higher risk of cardiovascular events (especially ischaemic heart disease events) than women at all ages. The reasons for this are unclear but may include their higher haematocrit (and hence blood viscosity and platelet adhesion or aggregation) from puberty onwards [10] and their lower levels of high density lipoprotein (HDL) cholesterol, which may be 'cardioprotective' [15]. Nevertheless, in women over the age of 60 years, ischaemic heart disease is the primary cause of death and one in four women, as well as one in four men, die of ischaemic heart disease after this age. In general, risk assessment and secondary prevention should be similar in men and women, although women have an added potential benefit from hormone replacement therapy.

Family history
Family history of premature cardiovascular disease is a risk factor that may partly operate through genetic influences on dyslipidaemia, hypertension, insulin resistance and fibrinogen but social factors such as smoking and diet must also be taken into account.

Smoking
Recent studies have shown that the effect of cigarette smoking on health has been underestimated: most smokers die because their smoking has caused premature cardiovascular disease or cancer [16]. Smoking is the leading preventable cause of death in developed countries and is increasing in developing countries. The impact of smoking on premature MI is particularly strong and is little affected by use of low-tar cigarettes [14]. Smoking shows an even stronger association with peripheral arterial disease than with ischaemic heart disease [17] and is also associated with both ischaemic and haemorrhagic stroke [18]. Few randomized trials of smoking cessation in primary prevention have been made and their results were disappointing, perhaps because the strongest predictor of risk is lifetime exposure (smoking-years) [19]. Nevertheless, smoking is an accepted risk factor because of its strong, consistent and dose-dependent associations with cardiovascular disease, the decline in risk over several years after cessation of smoking and the biological plausibility of its effects on the cardiovascular

system. These include effects on rheological and thrombotic mechanisms [10,20], including plasma fibrinogen, which has been shown to account for much of the association between smoking and ischaemic heart disease [20]. Smoking may induce arterial endothelial cell damage, through which the increasing plasma fibrinogen infiltrates the arterial wall [20]. After smoking cessation, fibrinogen levels stabilize in parallel with reduction in ischaemic heart disease risk (Fig. 2.1) [19,20].

Smoking retains its predictive power for cardiovascular events after the onset of clinically detectable arterial disease. The risk of recurrent MI falls after smoking cessation [21–24], as does the risk of progression of peripheral arterial disease [25–27]. Evidence indicates that stopping or reducing smoking is the most important lifestyle modification in secondary prevention of arterial disease. Smoking is also a risk factor for occlusion of coronary and peripheral arterial bypass grafts and stopping or reducing smoking is important in prevention [28–30].

Serum lipids and lipoproteins
Increasing serum total cholesterol levels in the general population (which are largely determined by low density lipoprotein [LDL] cholesterol) are predictive of ischaemic heart disease (Fig. 2.2) [3,31] and are associated with peripheral arterial disease [12] and ischaemic stroke [4]. The association is strong, consistent and dose-dependent and increased serum cholesterol has biologically plausible atherogenic [7] and other effects [8] that promote cardiovascular events.

Like smoking, serum cholesterol retains its predictive power for cardiovascular events after the onset of clinically detectable ischaemic heart disease (Figs 2.3 and 2.4) [8,32–38].

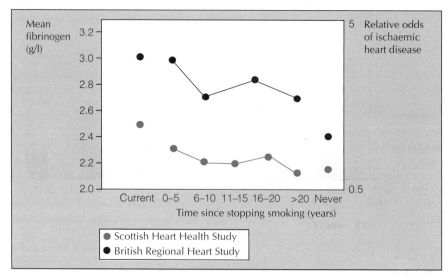

Fig. 2.1. *Effects of smoking cessation on age-standardized plasma fibrinogen levels (Scottish Heart Health Study) and on risk of ischaemic heart disease (age-standardized relative odds; British Regional Heart Study). Adapted with permission from Lowe [20].*

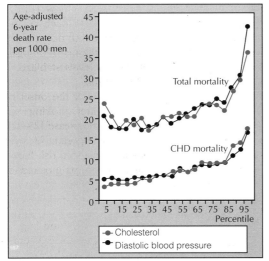

Fig. 2.2. *Relationships of serum total cholesterol and diastolic blood pressure to ischaemic heart disease and total mortality in the MRFIT study. Adapted with permission from Martin et al. [31].*

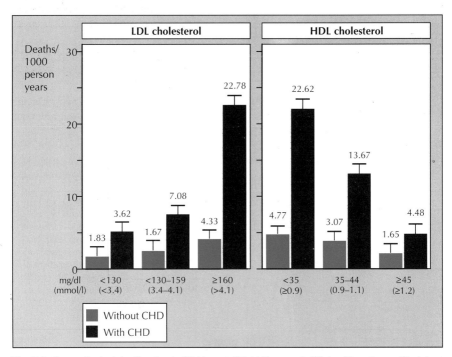

Fig. 2.3. *Age-adjusted death rates in 2541 men (Lipid Research Clinics Prevalence Study). Risk of death increases with increasing LDL cholesterol and with decreasing HDL cholesterol. However, the absolute risks are much higher in those with clinical CHD. Adapted with permission from Pekkanen et al. [36].*

17

More importantly, randomized controlled trials of cholesterol lowering in secondary prevention of cardiovascular events have shown reductions not only in ischaemic heart disease mortality and cardiovascular mortality but also in all-cause mortality [37–39]. In Figure 2.5, the apparently neutral effects of cholesterol reduction on noncardiovascular mortality (due to cancer or other causes) are shown [39]. Evidence from the trials performed before 1990 [37–39] has been supported by the 4S study, in which simvastatin treatment was shown to reduce total and cholesterol levels by 25 and 35% respectively, increase HDL cholesterol levels by 8% and reduce nonfatal MI by 37%, revascularization procedures by 37%, ischaemic heart disease deaths by 42% and, most importantly, total mortality by 30% [40]. Together with evidence that cholesterol reduction slows the progression of atherosclerosis [7,8], these data strongly support the case for cholesterol reduction by diet or drugs not only in patients with angina or previous MI but also in those with peripheral arterial disease, ischaemic strokes or transient ischaemic attacks — many such patients have both coronary atherosclerosis and peripheral atherosclerosis. Cholesterol is predictive of coronary artery graft occlusion [41] and cholesterol reduction reduces postgraft atherosclerosis [42].

Risk of ischaemic heart disease is associated inversely with serum HDL cholesterol levels. As with total and LDL cholesterol, its impact is greater in patients with established ischaemic heart disease than in those without (see Fig. 2.3) [36]. This inverse association is particularly strong in women [15]. Low HDL cholesterol levels are related to smoking, lack of exercise and other aspects of the insulin resistance syndrome (truncal obesity, triglyceride, hypertension, impaired glucose tolerance and hyperinsulinaemia). HDL cholesterol levels also show inverse associations with restenosis after coronary angioplasty [43].

Whether triglyceride is an independent risk factor for cardiovascular events is still debated. Recent studies suggest that the combination of high triglyceride and low HDL cholesterol, even without high LDL cholesterol, is predictive of MI [44]. Such individuals often have other features of the insulin resistance syndrome [45]. In part, this increased risk of ischaemic heart disease may be due to the presence of small LDL subfractions, which are more atherogenic [46] but which are not routinely measured in biochemistry laboratories.

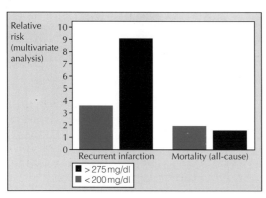

Fig. 2.4. *Relative risks of recurrent ischaemic heart disease after MI in individuals with cholesterol > 275 mg/dl (7.1 mmol/l) relative to those with cholesterol < 200 mg/dl (5.2 mmol/l). Adapted with permission from Wong et al. [34].*

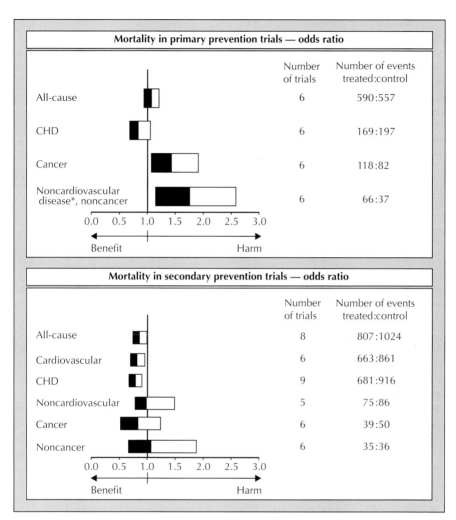

Fig. 2.5. *Mortality in primary and secondary prevention trials. *Accidents, violence, trauma, suicide. Adapted with permission from La Rosa [39].*

Blood pressure

As for serum total cholesterol, increasing blood pressure levels (systolic, diastolic or mean) are predictive of ischaemic heart disease (see Fig. 2.2) [31,47] and the association with peripheral arterial disease is similar [12,48]. The associations with stroke and with heart failure are stronger [47,48], probably because the mechanical effects of blood pressure on intracranial small-vessel disease (causing aneurysmal haemorrhage or lacunar infarction) and on the left ventricle, respectively, are added to its atherogenic effects.

Meta-analysis of the randomized primary prevention trials of blood pressure lowering by drugs showed a worthwhile reduction in stroke (42%) but little reduction in ischaemic heart disease (14%) [5]. Hence, drug treatment of hypertension has been recommended in high-risk patients, such as those with multiple risk factors, the elderly and those with cardiovascular disease.

Concern has been expressed that lowering blood pressure below a certain level may increase the risk of cardiovascular events — the 'J-shaped curve' — especially in patients with clinically evident arterial disease, such as ischaemic heart disease [49]. However, the authors of a recent review concluded that such a curve is probably a consequence rather than a cause of ischaemic heart disease and declining left ventricular function and they recommended that blood pressure can be lowered to 125/85 mmHg [50].

Blood pressure lowering drugs vary widely in their effects on the cardiovascular system and other cardiovascular risk factors [51]. Hence the type of drug is important, in interpretation of clinical trials and in choice of drug for individual patients.

Both beta-adrenergic blockers and angiotensin converting enzyme (ACE) inhibitors have been shown to reduce mortality in patients who have survived MI. ACE inhibitors also reduce the risk of heart failure in patients with major ventricular dysfunction. Nitrovasodilators appear to have no effect on mortality and an effect of calcium antagonists on mortality is disputed [52].

In angina pectoris, drugs that reduce both anginal episodes and blood pressure, for example beta-adrenergic blockers and calcium antagonists, may be preferred [53], although short-acting dihydropyridine calcium antagonists might increase mortality [54].

In peripheral arterial disease, hypertension increases mortality but does not increase risk of deterioration in leg ischaemia [55]. Beta blockers may reduce leg blood flow and walking distance, especially in combination with nifedipine [56]. Patients with claudications also have a high prevalence of renal artery stenosis at angiography [57], which may lead to renal hypoperfusion after use of ACE inhibitors.

In patients with stroke or transient cerebral ischaemic attacks, control of hypertension (reduction of diastolic blood pressure < 100mmHg) reduces the risk of recurrent stroke [58]. However, immediate hypotensive therapy in acute stroke is hazardous because of impairment of cerebral blood flow and further cerebral infarction. Similarly, hypotensive therapy should be given with caution in patients with severe carotid stenosis.

Obesity

Obesity is a prime cause of dyslipidaemia, hypertension and glucose intolerance. Weight loss through diet and exercise is the first-line treatment of these cardiovascular risk factors. Obesity is a strong and biologically plausible risk factor for cardiovascular disease and mortality, largely through the above mechanisms [59,60]. Abdominal obesity appears to confer a higher risk than overall obesity [15]. Although weight loss reduces blood pressure, dyslipidaemia and glucose intolerance, limited compliance means that direct evidence that weight reduction reduces the risk of cardiovascular disease is lacking. Nevertheless, weight loss should be advised in obese persons with evident cardiovascular disease, not only to reduce risk factors but also to reduce cardiac demands on exercise, which may lead to improvement in angina or claudication.

Lack of exercise

Lack of exercise is associated with increased risk of ischaemic heart disease [15,61], stroke [62] and peripheral arterial disease [63]. Its effects may be mediated partly through obesity, dyslipidaemia (decreased HDL cholesterol), hypertension and glucose intolerance. As with obesity, limited compliance results in a lack of evidence that increased exercise reduces the risk of cardiovascular disease [15]. However, exercise should be encouraged in sedentary individuals with evident cardiovascular disease, not only to reduce risk factors but also to improve exercise performance after MI [52] and in claudication [64].

Diabetes mellitus

The associations of insulin resistance and glucose intolerance with cardiovascular disease, obesity, hypertension and dyslipidaemia have been discussed earlier. Patients with diabetes carry a higher risk of cardiovascular events (men, relative risk 2–4;24 women, relative risk 3–7) [15]. Increased risk in women may be partly because diabetes impairs oestrogen binding, negating the protection conferred by endogenous oestrogens in premenopausal women. Risk factor modification of smoking, hypertension and obesity yields greater reductions in absolute risk of cardiovascular events in diabetic than in nondiabetic patients. Intensive treatment of insulin-dependent diabetic patients appears to slow the development of other diabetic complications.

Alcohol consumption

Increasing evidence that moderate alcohol consumption reduces the risk of ischaemic heart disease and stroke has led to recent reconsiderations of previously recommended 'safe limits of drinking': 21 units (8 g ethanol) per week for men and 14 units per week for women [65]. This apparent protective effect may reflect increased HDL cholesterol, decreased platelet aggregation and fibrinogen and increased tissue plasminogen activator release [15]. However, alcohol increases the risks of injury, liver disease, and certain cancers, in addition to increasing haemorrhagic stroke, heart failure, triglyceride levels and plasminogen activator inhibitor release. In men and women aged less than 40 years, alcohol consumption increases total mortality, even at low levels of consumption, and, in countries with low ischaemic heart disease rates, such as Japan, mortality from haemorrhagic stroke is high [65]. Maintaining current 'safe limits' seems appropriate, as does emphasising that these may be appropriate only from middle-age onwards in industrialized countries and that binge drinking should be avoided.

Fat consumption

Comparisons between countries have shown a triangular association between dietary saturated fat, serum cholesterol and ischaemic heart disease, both epidemiologically [66] and in necropsy studies of the extent of coronary atherosclerosis [67]. Reduction in dietary saturated fat and cholesterol and increase in polyunsaturated fat reduces serum LDL cholesterol levels, although compliance with such recommended diets in the general population is limited [68]. Advice to eat fatty fish in patients after MI is associated with a small reduction in mortality but an increase in nonfatal

21

reinfarction [69]. Advice to eat fruit and reduce fat was associated with a relative risk reduction of 59% in mortality and 48% in reinfarction, compared with fat reduction alone [70].

Haematological variables

Rheology

Interest in haematological factors is relatively recent [10,20,71]. Increased haematocrit has been associated with cardiovascular events in several studies [10]. Recent long-term reports [72–74] confirm its independent prediction of ischaemic heart disease and stroke. Plasma viscosity is an independent predictor of ischaemic heart disease and may be one mechanism through which increased fibrinogen levels promote ischaemia [75]. Blood viscosity is determined mainly by haematocrit and plasma viscosity but also by erythrocyte deformability and aggregation. It has been associated with peripheral arterial disease [76], ischaemic heart disease [77] and hypertension [78,79] in cross-sectional studies but prospective data are awaited. Erythrocyte aggregation, measured by the erythrocyte sedimentation rate, is also a predictor of cardiovascular events [80,81] and may be another rheological mechanism through which fibrinogen promotes ischaemia. Investigators in several studies have shown that increased leucocyte count is also a predictor of ischaemic heart disease and stroke [10], partly because of the rheological effects of neutrophils and monocytes in occluding capillaries in ischaemic heart, brain and skeletal muscle. Increased plasma viscosity, erythrocyte aggregation and leucocyte count also predict recurrent ischaemic events in unstable angina [82,83] and after recovery from MI [84,85] or stroke [86].

No large controlled trials of modification of these haemorheological variables have yet been performed and their role as risk factors remains to be established.

Haemostatic variables

Platelet-fibrin thrombi continuously form haemostatic plugs, venous thrombi in the leg veins and mural aortic and arterial thrombi, from early adult life onwards [71]. Thrombosis not only contributes to atherogenesis but also precipitates the most clinically important arterial events, either by thrombus formation on ruptured arterial or aortic plaques [87] or by embolizing from the heart, most often in atrial fibrillation [88]. Many studies of haemostatic variables have been performed in recent years, and these have recently been reviewed in detail [10,71].

Platelet count, volume or aggregation predict ischaemic heart disease events in the few studies that have been reported [85,89,90]. The role of platelet aggregation in thrombosis has been shown by the beneficial effects in large controlled trials of aspirin, ticlopidine and dipyridamole [52].

Von Willebrand factor, released largely from endothelial cells, mediates platelet adhesion to subendothelium and platelet aggregation at high shear rates. It also stabilizes coagulation factor VIII in the circulation. Increased levels of von Willebrand factor and factor VIII are predictive of ischaemic heart disease events [91–94]. Anti-von Willebrand factor drugs are currently being evaluated in thrombosis and the results of these trials may illuminate its role in thrombosis, which appears to be important in experimental studies.

The predictive value of coagulation factor VIII for ischaemic heart disease appears most marked for fatal events. Its biological importance is suggested by the low risk of ischaemic heart disease (relative risk 0.2) in factor VIII deficiency (haemophilia A) [91]. Factor VII is also a predictor of ischaemic heart disease, again particularly of fatal events [95,96]. Its biological role is being assessed in trials of low-dose warfarin in men with high factor VII levels: the efficacy of warfarin in prevention of recurrent MI is consistent with such a role [52].

Fibrinogen is a strong, consistent and dose-dependent predictor of ischaemic heart disease, stroke and peripheral arterial disease. Its potential role as a cardiovascular risk factor has recently been reviewed [20,71,97]. Eight prospective studies in initially healthy populations have consistently shown fibrinogen to predict both ischaemic heart disease events and mortality in men and women (Fig. 2.6) [98,99]. Investigators in several studies have suggested that much of the effect of cigarette smoking on arterial disease is mediated by fibrinogen (see Fig. 2.1) [20,71,76]. Fibrinogen and cholesterol show an important interaction in risk of ischaemic heart disease [93,95] and fibrinogen and blood pressure also show an important interaction in risk of stroke [100]. Fibrinogen may form a link between infection and cardiovascular events, including dental infections [101], winter infections [102], *Helicobacter* gastritis [103] and *Chlamydia* pneumonia [103].

Fibrinogen also predicts recurrent cardiovascular events in unstable or stable angina [89,93], in claudication [17,104] and after recovery from MI [85] or stroke [86]. Fibrinogen may promote arterial disease by infiltration of the arterial wall, platelet aggregation, fibrin thrombus formation, decreased thrombus lysability or its rheological effects on plasma and blood viscosity [20,71,97]. Its biological role is being assessed in large controlled trials of fibrates such as bezafibrate, which lowers plasma fibrinogen levels by about 25% [97].

Cross-linked fibrin degradation products, an index of fibrin turnover which is usually measured as fibrin D-dimer, have been shown to predict progression of peripheral arterial disease [17], and ischaemic heart disease events in claudicants [17] and apparently healthy men [92,105]. Decreased fibrinolytic potential of blood, measured as prolonged dilute whole blood clot lysis times, was recently reported to predict ischaemic heart disease in younger men [106], possibly because of increased levels of plasminogen activator inhibitor, which predicted recurrent MI in younger men [107]. However, other studies of plasminogen activator inhibitor activity have not shown independent prediction of ischaemic heart disease [92,108], nor have studies of tissue plasminogen activator antigen, which is complexed to plasminogen activator inhibitor [93,109]. In other studies, tissue plasminogen activator antigen levels were predictive of stroke [110] and of cardiac events in unstable angina [93].

The association of other haemostatic variables (coagulation inhibitors, factor XII deficiency, lupus anticoagulants) with cardiovascular disease remains uncertain [71].

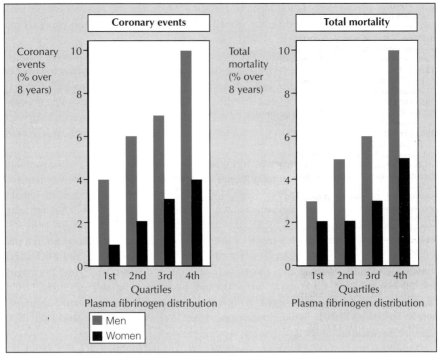

Fig. 2.6. *Fibrinogen levels predict both ischaemic heart disease events and mortality in men and women. Adapted with permission from Lowe [99].*

References

1. Heller RF *et al.*: **How well can we predict coronary heart disease?** *BMJ* 1984, **288**:1409–1411.
2. Davey-Smith G *et al.*: **Cholesterol lowering and mortality: importance of considering initial level of risk.** *BMJ* 1992, **306**:1367–1373.
3. West RR: **Cholesterol screening: can it be justified?** *Hospital Update* 1995:219–228.
4. Warlow CP: **Epidemiology of stroke.** In *Textbook of Vascular Medicine.* Edited by Tooke JE, Lowe GDO. London: Edward Arnold; 1996, in press.
5. Collins R *et al.*: **Blood pressure, stroke and coronary heart disease. 2. Short-term reductions in blood pressure: overview of randomised drug trials in their epidemiological context.** *Lancet* 1990, **335**:827–838.
6. Multiple Risk Factor Intervention Trial Research Group: **Mortality rates after 10.5 years for participants in the Multiple Risk Factor Intervention Trial.** *JAMA* 1990, **263**:1795–1801.
7. La Rosa JC: **Cholesterol lowering, low cholesterol,** and mortality. *Am J Cardiol* 1993, **72**:776–786.
8. Levine GN *et al.*: **Cholesterol reduction in cardiovascular disease. Clinical benefits and possible mechanisms.** *N Engl J Med* 1995, **332**:512–521.
9. Treasure CB *et al.*: **Beneficial effects of cholesterol-lowering therapy on the coronary endothelium in patients with coronary artery disease.** *N Engl J Med* 1995, **332**:481–487.
10. Lowe GDO. **Blood rheology, haemostasis and vascular disease.** In *Haemostasis and Thrombosis*, 3rd edition. Edited by Bloom AL *et al.* Edinburgh: Churchill Livingstone; 1994:1169–1188.
11. Gordon T, Kannel WB: **Predisposition to atherosclerosis in the head, heart and legs. The Framingham Study.** *JAMA* 1972, **221**:661–666.
12. Fowkes FGR: **Epidemiology of peripheral arterial disease.** In *Textbook of Vascular Medicine.* Edited by Tooke JE, Lowe GDO. London: Edward Arnold; 1996, in press.

13. Bradford Hill A: **The environment and disease: association or causation?** *Proc R Soc Med* 1965, **58**: 295–300.

14. Parish S *et al.*: **Cigarette-smoking, tar yields, and non-fatal myocardial infarction: 14000 cases and 32000 controls in the United Kingdom.** *BMJ* 1995, **311**:471–477.

15. Rich-Edwards JW *et al.*: **The primary prevention of coronary heart disease in women.** *N Engl J Med* 1995, **332**:1758–1766.

16. Doll R *et al.*: **Mortality in relation to smoking: 40 years observations on male British doctors.** *BMJ* 1994, **309**:901–911.

17. Fowkes FGR *et al.*: **Smoking, lipids, glucose intolerance, and blood pressure as risk factors for peripheral atherosclerosis compared with ischaemic heart disease in the Edinburgh Artery Study.** *Am J Epidemiol* 1992, **135**:331–340.

18. Shinton R, Beevers G: **Meta-analysis of relation between cigarette smoking and stroke.** *BMJ* 1989, **298**:789–794.

19. Cook DG *et al.*: **Giving up smoking and the risk of heart attacks.** *Lancet* 1986, **ii**:1376–1389.

20. Lowe GDO: *The Impact of Fibrinogen on Arterial Disease.* Amsterdam: Excerpta Medica, 1993.

21. Wilhelmsen C *et al.*: **Smoking and myocardial infarction.** *Lancet* 1975, **i**:415–420.

22. Sparrow D *et al.*: **The influence of cigarette smoking on prognosis after a first myocardial infarction.** *J Chron Dis* 1978, **31**:425–432.

23. Daly LC *et al.*: **Long term effect on mortality of stopping smoking after unstable angina and myocardial infarction.** *BMJ* 1983, **287**:324–326.

24. Vlietsra RE *et al.*: **Effect of cigarette smoking on survival of patients with angiographically documented coronary artery disease.** *JAMA* 1986, **255**:1023–1027.

25. Jonason T, Bergstrom R: **Cessation of smoking in patients with intermittent claudication.** *Acta Med Scand* 1987, **221**:253–260.

26. Jonason T, Ringqvist I: **Changes in peripheral blood pressures after five years of follow-up in non-operated patients with intermittent claudication.** *Acta Med Scand* 1986, **220**:127–132.

27. Fowkes FG *et al.*: **Cross-linked fibrin degradation products, progression of peripheral arterial disease, and risk of coronary heart disease.** *Lancet* 1993, **342**:84–86.

28. Cavender JB *et al.*: **Effects of smoking on survival and morbidity in patients randomised to medical or surgical therapy in the Coronary Artery Surgery Study (CASS): 10-year follow-up.** *J Am Coll Cardiol* 1992, **20**:287–294.

29. Wiseman S *et al.*: **Influence of smoking and plasma factors on patency of femoropopliteal vein grafts.** *BMJ* 1989, **299**:643–646.

30. Greenhalgh RM: **The effect of smoking on arterial disease and venous thrombosis.** In *Surgical Management of Vascular Disease.* Edited by Bell PRF, Jamieson CW, Ruckley CV. London: WB Saunders, 1991:103–109.

31. Martin MJ *et al.*: **Serum cholesterol, blood pressure, and mortality.** *Lancet* 1986, **ii**:933–936.

32. Hagman M *et al.*: **Factors of importance for prognosis in men with angina pectoris derived from a random population sample: the Multifactor Primary Prevention trial, Gothenburg, Sweden.** *Am J Cardiol* 1988, **61**:530–535.

33. Philips AN *et al.*: **The role of risk factors in heart attacks occurring in men with preexisting ischaemic heart disease.** *Br Heart J* 1988, **60**:404–410.

34. Wong ND *et al.*: **Risk factors for long-term coronary prognosis after initial myocardial infarction: the Framingham Study.** *Am J Epidemiol* 1989, **130**:469–480.

35. Philips AN, Shaper AG: **Secondary prevention of coronary heart disease.** *Lancet* 1989, **i**:718–719.

36. Pekkanen J *et al.*: **Ten-year mortality from cardiovascular disease in relation to cholesterol level among men with and without pre-existing cardiovascular disease.** *N Engl J Med* 1990, **322**:1700–1707.

37. Rossouw JE *et al.*: **The value of lowering cholesterol after myocardial infarction.** *N Engl J Med* 1990, **323**:1112–1119.

38. Rossouw JE *et al.*: **Deaths from injury, violence, and suicide in secondary prevention trials of cholesterol lowering.** *N Engl J Med* 1991, **325**: 1813–1815.

39. La Rosa JC: *Secondary Prevention of Coronary Heart Disease: Altering Lipoproteins.* Amsterdam: Excerpta Medica, 1993.

40. Scandinavian Simvastatin Survival Study Group: **Randomised trial of cholesterol lowering in 4444 patients with coronary heart disease: the 4S Study.** *Lancet* 1994, **344**:1383–1389.

41. Campeau L *et al.*: **The relation of risk factors to the development of atherosclerosis in saphenous-vein bypass grafts and the progression of disease in the native circulation.** *N Engl J Med* 1984, **311**:1329–1332.

42. Blankenhorn DH *et al.*: **Beneficial effects of combined colestipol-niacin therapy on coronary atherosclerosis and coronary venous bypass grafts.** *JAMA* 1987, **257**:323–3240.

43. Shah PK, Amin J: **Low high density lipoprotein level is associated with increased restenosis rate after coronary angioplasty.** *Circulation* 1992, **85**:1279–1285.

44. Assman G *et al.*: **The Prospective Cardiovascular Münster (PROCAM) Study: identification of high-risk individuals for myocardial infarction and the role of HDL.** In *High Density Lipoproteins and Atherosclerosis II.* Edited by Miller NE. Amsterdam: Elsevier; 1989: 51–65.

45. Godsland I *et al.*: **Insulin resistance: syndrome or tendency?** *Lancet* 1995, **346**:100–103.

46. Rajman I *et al.*: **Particle size: the key to the atherogenic lipoprotein?** *QJM* 1994, **87**:709–720.

47. MacMahon S *et al.*: **Blood pressure, stroke and coronary heart disease. 1. Prolonged differences in blood pressure: prospective observational studies corrected for the regression dilution bias.** *Lancet* 1990, **335**:765–776.

48. Kannel WB: **Epidemiology of essential hypertension: the Framingham experience.** *Proc R Coll Physicians Edinb* 1991, **21**:273–287.

49. Cruickshank JM: **Coronary flow reserve and the J curve: relation between diastolic blood pressure and myocardial infarction.** *BMJ* 1988, **297**:1227–1230.

50. Fletcher AE, Bulpitt CJ: **How far should blood pressure be lowered?** *N Engl J Med* 1992, **326**: 251–254.

51. Dzau VJ *et al.*: **Hypertension: evaluation and management.** In *Vascular Medicine.* Edited by Loscalzo J *et al.* Boston: Little, Brown; 1992: 595–657.

52. Cleland JGF: **Overview of large clinical trials in patients with myocardial infarction.** In *Preventative Strategies after Myocardial Infarction.* Edited by Cleland J *et al.* London: Science Press; 1994: 37–73.

53. Frohlich ED *et al.*: **The heart in hypertension.** *N Engl J Med* 1992, **327**:998–1008.

54. Furberg CD *et al.*: **Nifedipine. Dose-related increase in mortality in patients with coronary heart disease.** *Circulation* 1995, **92**:1326–1331.

55. Dormandy JA, Murray GD: **The fate of the claudicant – a prospective study of 1969 claudicants.** *Eur J Vasc Surg* 1991, **5**:131–133.

56. Solomon SA *et al.*: **Beta-blockade and intermittent claudication: placebo controlled trial of atenolol and nifedipine and their combination.** *BMJ* 1991, **303**:100–104.

57. Choudri AH *et al.*: **Unsuspected renal artery stenosis in peripheral vascular disease.** *BMJ* 1990, **301**:1197–1198.

58. Beevers DG *et al.*: **Antihypertensive treatment in the course of established cerebral vascular disease.** *Lancet* 1973, **i**:1407–1408.

59. Hubert HB *et al.*: **Obesity as an independent risk factor for cardiovascular disease: a 26 year follow-up of participants in the Framingham Heart Study.** *Circulation* 1983, **67**:968–977.

60. Manson JE *et al.*: **A prospective study of obesity and risk of coronary heart disease in women.** *N Engl J Med* 1990, **322**:882–889.

61. Berlin JA, Colditz GA: **A meta-analysis of physical activity in the prevention of coronary heart disease.** *Am J Epidemiol* 1990, **132**:612–628.

62. Wannamethee G *et al.*: **Physical activity and stroke in British middle-aged men.** *BMJ* 1992, **302**: 597–601.

63. Housley E: **Exercise.** In *Epidemiology of Peripheral Arterial Disease.* Edited by Fowkes FGR. London: Springer-Verlag; 1991:227–234.

64. Holm J: **The effect of exercise on intermittent claudication.** In *Surgical Management of Vascular Disease.* Edited by PRF Bell *et al.* London: WB Saunders; 1991:111–118.

65. Jackson R, Beaglehole R: **Alcohol consumption guidelines: relative safety vs absolute risks and benefits [Editorial].** *Lancet* 1995, **346**:716.

66. Keys A: *Seven Countries Study.* Cambridge, Mass: Howard University Press; 1980.

67. McGill HC Jr: *The Geographic Pathology of Atherosclerosis.* Baltimore: Williams and Wilkins; 1968.

68. Lewis B: **Diet and exercise as regulators of lipid risk factors.** *Drugs* 1990, **40**(suppl 1):19–25.

69. Burr M *et al.*: **Effects of changes in fat, fish and fibre intakes on death and myocardial reinfarction:**

Diet and Reinfarction Trial (DART). *Lancet* 1989, **ii**:757–761.

70. Singh RB *et al.*: **Randomised controlled trial of cardioprotective diet in patients with recent acute myocardial infarction: results on one year follow-up.** *BMJ* 1992, **304**:1015–1019.

71. Lowe GDO: **Haemostatic risk factors for arterial and venous thrombosis.** In *Recent Advances in Blood Coagulation,* edn 7. Edited by Poller L, Ludlam CA. Edinburgh: Churchill Livingstone, 1996.

72. Gagnon DR *et al.*: **Hematocrit and the risk of cardiovascular disease — the Framingham Study: a 34-year follow up.** *Am Heart J* 1994, **127**:674–682.

73. Wannamethee G *et al.*: **Ischaemic heart disease: association with haematocrit in the British Regional Heart Study.** *J Epid Commun Hlth* 1994, **48**:112–118.

74. Wannamethee G *et al.*: **Haematocrit, hypertension and risk of stroke.** *J Intern Med* 1994, **235**:163–168.

75. Yarnell JWG *et al.*: **Fibrinogen, viscosity and white blood cell count are major risk factors for ischaemic heart disease. The Caerphilly and Speedwell Collaborative Heart Disease Studies.** *Circulation* 1991, **83**:836–844.

76. Lowe GDO *et al.*: **Blood viscosity, fibrinogen and activation of coagulation and leukocytes in peripheral arterial disease and the normal population in the Edinburgh Artery Study.** *Circulation* 1993, **87**:1915–1920.

77. Lowe GDO *et al.*: **Blood rheology and haemostasis in survivors of premature myocardial infarction: a case-control study.** *Thromb Haemostas* 1993, **69**:796.

78. Smith WCS *et al.*: **Rheological determinants of blood pressure in a Scottish adult population.** *J Hypertens* 1992, **10**:467–472.

79. Fowkes FGR *et al.*: **Relation of blood viscosity to blood pressure in a random sample of the population aged 55–74 years.** *Eur Heart J* 1993, **14**:597–601.

80. Bottiger L, Carlson LA: **Risk factors for ischaemic vascular death for men in the Stockholm Prospective Study.** *Atherosclerosis* 1980, **36**:389–408.

81. Gillum RF *et al.*: **Erythrocyte sedimentation rate and coronary heart disease: the NHANES I epidemiologic follow-up study.** *J Clin Epidemiol* 1995, **48**:353–361.

82. Neumann F-J *et al.*: **Activation and decreased deformability of leukocytes in claudication.** *Circulation* 1991, **82**:922–929.

83. Fuchs J *et al.*: **Plasma viscosity, fibrinogen and haematocrit in the course of unstable angina.** *Eur Heart J* 1991, **11**:1029–1032.

84. Lowe GDO *et al.*: **White blood cell count and haematocrit as predictors of coronary recurrence after myocardial infarction.** *Thromb Haemostas* 1985, **54**:700–703.

85. Martin JF *et al.*: **Influence of platelet size on outcome after myocardial infarction.** *Lancet* 1991, **338**:1409–1411.

86. Ernst E *et al.*: **Impaired blood rheology: a risk factor after stroke?** *J Intern Med* 1991, **229**:457–462.

87. Davies MJ: **Thrombosis and coronary atherosclerosis.** In *Thrombolysis in cardiovascular disease.*

Edited by Julian D *et al.* Basel: Marcel Dekker; 1989:25–44.

88. Albers G: **Atrial fibrillation and stroke.** *Arch Intern Med* 1994, **154**:1143–1148.

89. Trip MD *et al.*: **Platelet hyperreactivity and prognosis in survivors of myocardial infarction.** *N Engl J Med* 1990, **322**:1549–1554.

90. Thaulow E *et al.*: **Blood platelet count and function are related to total and cardiovascular death in apparently healthy men.** *Circulation* 1991, **84**:613–617.

91. Meade TW *et al.*: **Factor VIII, ABO blood group and the incidence of ischaemic heart disease.** *Br J Haematol* 1994, **88**:601–607.

92. Lowe GDO *et al.*: **Fibrin D-dimer, von Willebrand factor, tissue plasminogen activator antigen, and plasminogen activator inhibitor activity are primary risk factors for ischaemic heart disease: the Caerphilly Study.** *Thromb Haemostas* 1995, **73**:950.

93. Thompson SG *et al.*: **Hemostatic factors and risk of myocardial infarction or sudden death in patients with angina pectoris. European Concerted Action on Thrombosis and Disabilities Angina Pectoris Study Group.** *N Engl J Med* 1995, **332**:635–641.

94. Woodburn KR *et al.*: **Predictive value of pre-operative plasma fibrinogen, fibrin degradation products, and von Willebrand factor for graft occlusion or death following infra-inguinal revascularisation surgery for peripheral arterial disease** [Abstract]. *Blood Coagul Fibrinolysis* 1994, **5(suppl 2)**:13.

95. Heinrich J *et al.*: **Fibrinogen and factor VII in the prediction of coronary risk. Results from the PROCAM study in healthy men.** *Arterioscler Thromb* 1994, **14**:54–59.

96. Ruddock V, Meade TW: **Factor VII activity and ischaemic heart disease: fatal and non-fatal events.** *QJM* 1994, **87**:403–406.

97. Lowe GDO *et al.*: **Fibrinogen and cardiovascular disease.** *Eur Heart J* 1995, **16(suppl A)**:2–5.

98. Ernst E, Resch KL: **Fibrinogen as a cardiovascular risk factor: a meta-analysis and review of the literature.** *Ann Intern Med* 1993, **118**:956–963.

99. Lowe GD: **Haematology and risk — a neglected link?** *Issues in Hyperlipidaemia, No 12.* Lancaster: Kluwer; 1996.

100. Wilhelmsen L *et al.*: **Fibrinogen as a risk factor for stroke and myocardial infarction.** *N Engl J Med* 1984, **311**:501–505.

101. Kweider M *et al.*: **Dental disease, fibrinogen and white cell count: links with myocardial infarction?** *Scott Med J* 1993, **38**:73–74.

102. Woodhouse PR *et al.*: **Seasonal variations of plasma fibrinogen and factor VII activity in the elderly: winter infections and death from cardiovascular disease.** *Lancet* 1994, **343**:435–439.

103. Patel P *et al.*: **Association of *Helicobacter pylori* and *Chlamydia pneumoniae* infections with coronary heart disease and cardiovascular risk factors.** *BMJ* 1995, **311**:711–714.

104. Banerjee AK *et al.*: **A six year prospective study of fibrinogen and other risk factors associated with mortality in stable claudicants.** *Thromb Haemostas* 1992, **68**:261–263.

105. Ridker PM *et al.*: **Plasma concentration of cross-linked fibrin degradation products (D-dimer) and the risk of future myocardial infarction among apparently healthy men.** *Circulation* 1994, **90**: 2236–2240.

106. Meade TW *et al.*: **Fibrinolytic activity, clotting factors and long-term incidence of ischaemic heart disease in the Northwick Park Heart Study.** *Lancet* 1993, **342**:1076–1079.

107. Hamsten A *et al.*: **Plasminogen activator inhibitor in plasma: risk factor for recurrent myocardial infarction.** *Lancet* 1987, **ii**:3–9.

108. Ridker PM *et al.*: **A prospective study of plasminogen activator inhibitor and the risk of future myocardial infarction** [Editorial]. *Circulation* 1992, **86(suppl I)**: I-35.

109. Ridker PM *et al.*: **Endogenous tissue-type plasminogen activator and risk of myocardial infarction.** *Lancet* 1993, **341**:1165–1168.

110. Ridker PM *et al.*: **Prospective study of endogenous tissue plasminogen activator and risk of stroke.** *Lancet* 1994, **343**:940–943.

Diagnosis of coronary artery disease and angina
Iain Findlay and Luciano Moretti

Introduction

In general terms, the principal aim of a state health care system is to provide clinical benefit requisite to patient need at the lowest possible cost. The effectiveness of cardiological investigation and treatment has come under close scrutiny [1], with considerable doubts about its cost effectiveness [1–6]. The attention of purchasers is now focused on alleged waste of resources, which has been described for coronary angiography [7–11], coronary artery bypass grafting (CABG) [12] (although recent evidence suggests that this is not the case [13]), thallium scanning [14,15] and percutaneous transluminal coronary angioplasty (PTCA) [16]. Patterson *et al.* [17] proposed six questions that must be asked about current diagnostic and management tools for patients with known or suspected CHD.

- Does the test provide unique information of value to a clinician that is not otherwise available? Can a complex test be replaced adequately by the clinical history, examination or a simpler test?

- What is the extent of interobserver and intraobserver error associated with interpreting the test? Can the test be interpreted consistently by one doctor, within a group of doctors and between different centres?

- How do the sensitivities and specificities for detection of CHD by different means compare with each other? One accurate, complex test might be better than a whole series of simpler but inaccurate ones.

- What patient selection criteria should be applied for each test? One test might be best for men and another for women.

- What is the extent of any incremental benefit obtained from the use of one test when the information obtained is compared with that available from other diagnostic tests? The accuracy of a complex test should be judged not by its accuracy in isolation but its accuracy over and above simpler tests.

- Where do the different tests fit in the overall scheme of diagnostic testing for CHD? How is theory best used in practice?

History

Angina pectoris is a medical term applied to the symptoms of certain types of chest pain: it is not a diagnosis. In a society where CHD remains the most common cause of death, a link may rapidly be made between chest pain and CHD by patients and this is often reinforced by their doctors. Clearly from patients attending cardiology out-patient clinics, this concept is often well established by the time the patient is referred and breaking this link is difficult and often almost impossible. This is unfortunate if the cause of the patient's chest pain is noncardiac, especially if an alternative, readily treatable diagnosis is not apparent.

As in all aspects of medicine, patient history is very important. Poor history taking is largely responsible for the diagnosis being missed and the patient's symptoms being falsely attributed to CHD. The description of symptoms may vary from patient to patient according to education, social condition, age, sex and previous medical history. The translation of the patient's symptoms to a diagnosis needs specific questioning to define the location, quality, duration, severity, frequency and provocative factors of chest discomfort.

Diamond and Forrester [18] divide chest pain into three categories for the purpose of analysis:

• Typical angina

• Atypical angina

• Nonanginal chest pain

Many criteria have been published to help categorize patients into these groups. One of the most useful, suggested by Patterson and Horowitz [19], is shown in Figure 3.1.

Chest pain is classified by the following criteria:
1. Precipitation by exercise

2. Brief duration

3. Prompt relief by rest or nitroglycerine

4. Substernal location

5. Radiation from chest to jaw, left arm or neck

6. Absence of other causes of pain

I. Typical angina pectoris	II. Atypical chest pain	III. Nonanginal chest pain
Criteria 1– 3 positive	Any two criteria positive	Only one criterion positive
Any four criteria positive	Only criteria 4 – 6 positive	

Fig. 3.1. Categorization of angina pectoris according to Patterson and Horowitz [19].

29

The description of the chest pain allows the clinician to make an intuitive estimate of the probability that the patient has underlying CHD. Use of certain components of that pain can also be used to assess prognosis, for example frequency, severity and amount of exertion required to precipitate pain. An experienced clinician can probably give a reasonably accurate assessment of both the type of pain and prognosis but, in this era of evidence-based medicine and increasing patient awareness, there is a demand for more tangible proof.

The probability of disease given the patient's symptoms is predicted in several reports. In their classic paper, Diamond and Forrester [18] recorded the results from an investigation of 4952 patients in a review of 17 papers. These figures were comparable to those reported by Gibson and Beller [20] in a review of four studies from 1966 to 1979 investigating 3317 patients (Fig. 3.2). The influence of age, sex and ECG status has also been quantified (Fig. 3.3) [18]. Thus, for the same symptoms, the likelihood of disease is strongly influenced by age and sex.

Once the symptoms are classified, past medical history and the presence of risk factors should be determined. The most important thing to ascertain is whether the patient has a history of heart attack, which makes the presence of CHD almost certain. The question then becomes not one of diagnosis but rather of risk factor assessment and prognosis. The resting ECG also contains significant diagnostic content, as Weiner *et al.* showed in a study of the CASS database (Fig. 3.4) [21]. The resting ECG is frequently normal in patients with CHD but is rarely so in patients with significant left ventricular dysfunction.

	Diamond and Forrester [18]		Gibson and Beller [20]
Symptom	No. of patients	% patients	% patients
Nonanginal chest pain	146/913	16	11
Atypical angina	963/1931	50	54
Typical angina	1874/2108	88	88

Fig. 3.2. *The prevalence of angiographic coronary artery disease in symptomatic patients.*

	Nonanginal pain		Atypical angina		Typical angina	
Age (years)	Men	Women	Men	Women	Men	Women
30–39	5.2	0.8	21.8	4.2	69.7	25.8
40–49	14.1	2.8	46.1	13.3	87.3	55.2
50–59	21.5	8.4	58.9	32.4	92.0	79.4
60–69	28.11	18.6	67.1	54.4	94.3	90.6

Fig. 3.3. *The prevalence of disease stratified by age and sex. Data from Diamond and Forrester [18].*

Sex and clinical history	Resting ST-segments and T-waves	Prevalence of CHD (%)
In men		
Typical angina (n = 620)	Normal	88
	Abnormal	95
Atypical angina (n = 594)	Normal	6
	Abnormal	79
Nonanginal chest pain (n = 251)	Normal	22
	Abnormal	21
In women		
Typical angina (n = 98)	Normal	58
	Abnormal	71
Atypical angina (n = 240)	Normal	35
	Abnormal	47
Nonanginal chest pain (n = 242)	Normal	6
	Abnormal	5

Fig. 3.4. *Probability of CHD in men and women with either normal or abnormal ECGs. Data from the CASS database [21].*

Approximately 30% of MIs are silent and, in the postinfarct patient, both the diagnostic and the prognostic values of the exercise test are reduced [22,23].

Risk factors

Although often used to predict patients at risk of cardiovascular events, risk factors can also be used to decide the probability that equivocal symptoms are associated with underlying coronary disease. Peripheral vascular disease is under-recognised as a marker for severe coronary artery disease: 30% of such patients have severe coronary artery disease and only 8% have normal coronary arteries [24].

Bayesian models for diagnosis

Pryor *et al.* [25] developed a nomogram based on the examination of 3627 symptomatic patients referred for coronary angiography over a 10-year period. This nomogram was assessed prospectively in 1811 patients (Fig. 3.5).

The clinical profile of the patient built up from the history, physical examination, risk factors and the ECG allows the first approach towards a diagnosis to be made [18, 26–31]. The clinical profile is not sufficient to make a diagnosis to the degree of certainty

31

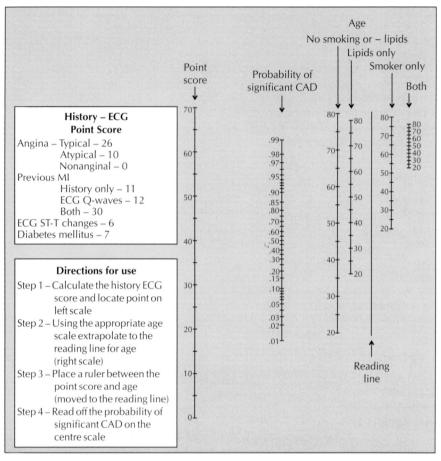

Fig 3.5. *A nomogram for estimating the probability of significant coronary artery disease (CAD) in women. A separate nomogram has been created for men. Adapted with permission from Pryor* et al. *[25].*

that would satisfy patient and doctor. At best it can determine high, intermediate and low probability of disease. Uncertainty of diagnosis is greatest for those patients with an intermediate probability of disease. The determination of the pretest probability of disease can be as simple as that based on symptom classification alone (see Figs 3.2–3.4) or can be more detailed, as in the probability available from the nomogram of Pryor *et al.* (see Fig. 3.5) [25].

This probability of disease is used with a diagnostic test to derive a post-test probability of disease. However, the sensitivity and specificity of the test being used must be known and many things affect these variables, principally the characteristics of the population used to derive them.

When a new diagnostic test is introduced, the sensitivity and specificity are often high but later investigators often report a decline in the accuracy of the test. This phenomenon was first reported for exercise radionuclide ventriculography in 1983 by Rozanski *et al.* [32] and was considered to be the result of selection bias. Pretest referral bias (preferential selection of patients on the basis of variables not related to disease, such as age and sex) can result in an unrepresentative population being tested. Posttest referral bias may have a greater influence if patients with a positive test are selected, for example for coronary angiography, in preference to those with a negative test. If a diagnostic test thought to be highly discriminant is used to screen patients for coronary angiography, it will suffer an apparent decline in specificity if the above selection pressures are applied. In the extreme case, if only patients with a positive test are catheterized, the sensitivity will be 100% because all patients with disease, selected for angiography on the basis of a positive test, will be detected. However, the specificity will be 0% because the remaining patients, all free of disease, also had a positive test as the basis on which they had angiography. Only by performing angiography on those with negative test results can the true sensitivity and specificity be estimated.

Gibson and Beller [20] used this bias to demonstrate the influence of population characteristics and their interaction with the sensitivity and specificity of the test used (Fig. 3.6).

In the example overleaf, a patient with a pretest probability of disease of 50%, undergoing an almost ideal test with a 92% sensitivity and 98% specificity, will have a post-test probability of disease of 98% if the test is positive and 7% (1–0.93) if the test is negative. The test shows great benefit in the diagnosis of CHD in those with an intermediate probability of disease. In those with high and low probabilities of disease, the test results are unhelpful, adding little to the pretest probability.

Unfortunately, the sensitivity and specificity of the exercise test do not approach that of the almost ideal test used in the above example. In Figure 3.7, the results obtained from meta-analysis of the 12-lead ECG in detecting significant CHD are shown.

If a satisfactory diagnostic certainty is not reached, the traditional approach would be to employ further tests, such as thallium scanning [14].

If we apply the results reported by Gianrossi (Fig. 3.7) [36] and use the sensitivity and specificity reported by Gould (Fig. 3.8) [37,38] of 70 and 68%, respectively, for thallium scanning to the patients with different pretest probabilities of disease, as shown in Figure 3.2, we find that a negative first test has reduced the probability of disease in a person with nonanginal chest pain from 11 to 4.89% and a negative second test reduces this further to 2.2% (Fig. 3.9). In the patient with typical symptoms and a high probability of disease (88%), a positive test increases the probability of disease from 95.6 to 97.9%.

In patients with an intermediate probability of disease with atypical chest pain, the pretest likelihood of 54 is raised to 77.6% with one positive test and to 88% with two positive tests. If both tests are negative, then the likelihood of disease falls from 54 to 17.3%. If diagnostic probabilities of more than 90% and less than 10% are defined as acceptable in confirming or refuting the presence of CHD, then, in a patient with atypical symptoms, at least two diagnostic tests are required to reach acceptable probabilities.

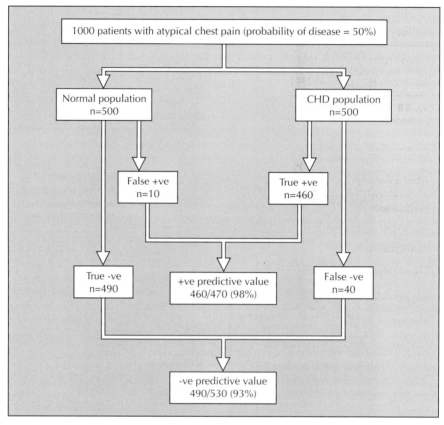

Fig. 3.6. *The determination of the probability of disease based on the pretest probability derived from clinical characteristics and a diagnostic test.*

Author	Years	No. of studies	No. of patients	Sensitivity (%)	Specificity (%)
Detrano [33,34]	1968–1969	10	5267	68	79
Gibson [20]	1976–1981	22	2048	58	82
Rozanski [35]	1975–1981	15	11 501	64	82
Detrano [33,34]	1974–1985	8	978	71	73
Gianrossi [36]	1967–1987	150	24 074	68	77

Fig. 3.7. *The reported sensitivity and specificity of stress ECG.*

Author	Year	No. of studies	No. of patients	Sensitivity (%)	Specificity (%)
Gibson [20]	1976–1981	22	2048	83 (ETT = 58%)	90 (ETT = 82%)
Gould [37,38]	1983–1994	8	4000	70	68

Fig. 3.8. *The reported sensitivity and specificity of thallium scintigraphy. ETT, exercise tolerance test.*

Description of pain	Pretest probability (%)	Post-test probability (%)	
		Stress ECG	Thallium testing
Positive tests			
Nonanginal	11	26.7	44.4
Atypical angina	54	77.6	88.3
Typical angina	88	95.6	97.9
Negative tests			
Nonanginal	11	4.9	2.2
Atypical angina	54	32.8	17.3
Typical angina	88	75.3	57.3

Fig. 3.9. *The post-test probability of disease using stress ECG, with sensitivity of 68% and specificity of 77%, and thallium scanning, with sensitivity of 70% and specificity of 68%, in patients with positive and negative tests (n = 1000).*

What level of uncertainty is acceptable to the patient, doctor and purchaser? Both the patient and the doctor may wish to confirm or exclude the presence of CHD, because this has psychological and management implications, but the purchaser may not have the same imperative to establish this if other factors suggest that, irrespective of the cause of symptoms, the prognosis is excellent. Superficially, this graded approach looks cost-effective as one proceeds through tests of increasing expense but a case could be made by a purchaser for stopping after a defined diagnostic probability has been reached. This may result in a refusal to sanction coronary angiography in a patient with an intermediate to high probability of disease if other factors suggest that, irrespective of the cause of the symptoms, the prognosis is excellent. An example from clinical practice might be a woman presenting with troublesome atypical chest pain but with a good effort capacity. However, the most cost-effective strategy in this instance could be to proceed directly to coronary angiography because clinical experience suggests that this will be a recurring problem that usually results in coronary angiography [31]. Pretest probability can be refined further by including the presence of resting ECG abnormalities and patient sex.

Age (years)	ST-segment depression (mm)	Typical angina		Possible or atypical angina		Nonspecific or nonanginal chest pain		Asymptomatic	
		M	W	M	W	M	W	M	W
30–39	0.0–0.4	25	7	6	1	1	<1	<1	<1
	0.5–0.9	68	24	21	4	5	1	2	<1
	1.0–1.4	83	42	38	9	10	2	4	<1
	1.5–1.9	91	59	55	15	19	3	7	1
	2.0–2.4	96	79	76	33	39	8	18	3
	>2.5	99	93	92	63	68	24	43	11
40–49	0.0–0.4	61	22	16	3	4	1	1	<1
	0.5–0.9	86	53	44	12	13	3	5	1
	1.0–1.4	94	72	64	25	26	6	11	2
	1.5–1.9	97	84	78	39	41	11	20	4
	2.0–2.4	99	93	91	63	65	24	39	10
	>2.5	>99	98	97	86	87	53	69	28
50–59	0.0–0.4	73	47	25	10	6	2	2	1
	0.5–0.9	91	78	57	31	20	8	9	3
	1.0–1.4	96	89	75	50	37	16	19	7
	1.5–1.9	98	94	86	67	53	28	31	12
	2.0–2.4	99	98	94	84	75	50	54	27
	>2.5	>99	99	98	95	91	78	81	56
60–69	0.0–0.4	79	69	32	21	8	5	3	2
	0.5–0.9	94	90	65	52	26	17	11	7
	1.0–1.4	97	95	81	72	45	33	23	15
	1.5–1.9	99	98	89	83	62	49	37	25
	2.0–2.4	99	99	96	93	81	72	61	47
	>2.5	>99	>99	99	98	94	90	85	73

Fig. 3.10. *Probability (%) of coronary artery disease based on sex, symptom classification and exercise induced ST-segment depression. M, men; W, women. Adapted with permission from Ascoop* et al. *[43].*

ST-segment and T-wave abnormalities are so powerful in raising the probability of disease in men with typical symptoms that further testing is not required, because a positive result adds only marginally to the pretest probability.

More information can be obtained from a test than whether it is positive or negative [39–43]. Additional information is conveyed by knowledge of the patient's age and by the extent of ST-segment depression during exercise. Ascoop *et al.* [43] published a detailed and useful classification incorporating these variables with symptom classification (Fig. 3.10). This refinement greatly reduces the numbers of patients in whom a second test is required.

The diagnostic accuracy of stress testing is lower in women than in men [44,45], reflecting in part the lower probability of disease in women. This phenomenon is not confined to stress ECG and has been reported for thallium scanning and radionuclide ventriculography. Allen *et al.* [46] followed up 888 asymptomatic individuals for 5 years after maximal stress test. The sensitivity and specificity were low in men and women, reflecting the low incidence of disease. In women, a poor effort capacity (< 3 min on the Ellestad protocol) was the only predictor of subsequent coronary events, whereas in men over the age of 40 years, ST-segment changes were predictive of subsequent coronary events. Therefore, the diagnostic criteria for abnormalities may be different in men and women. Manga *et al.* [47] evaluated 508 women and 947 men with atypical chest pain. After 3–7 years of follow-up, a positive stress test was associated with the development of clinical CHD in 18% of men and 5% of women. Barolsky *et al.* [48] studied men and women with a comparable prevalence of disease. The predictive value of a positive stress ECG was higher in men than in women (77% versus 47%), although the predictive value of a negative test was similar. Thus the diagnostic accuracy is lower in women, even in the presence of comparable disease prevalence.

Robert *et al.* [49] used multivariate analysis of exercise test data and found that work load, heart rate and ST-segment depression present in lead X of the orthogonal Frank lead system raised the sensitivity of stress ECG to about 70% without loss of specificity (about 90%).

Alternative diagnostic tests

Many tests other than the frequently used stress ECG are available.

Thallium scanning

The sensitivity and specificity reported for thallium scanning show the same variability and fall in overall accuracy with less highly selected populations as that reported by Rozanski [32] for radionuclide scanning (see Fig. 3.8). Single photon emission computed tomography myocardial perfusion imaging has advantages over planar thallium imaging, for example three-dimensional images and reduced image artefact. The place of thallium imaging compared with stress ECG remains unclear because differing sensitivities and specificities have been reported [17,38].

Radionuclide ventriculography

In a review of 76 papers published between 1979 and 1985 (unpublished data, Findlay IN and Cunningham AD), we found that failure of the left ventricular ejection fraction to rise by more than 5 units predicted the presence of angiographic coronary artery disease with 80% sensitivity and 84% specificity. A study population of 3004 patients with CHD and 1936 normal controls or patients with normal coronary arteries was investigated. Considerable overlap occurred in the mean resting left ventricular ejection fraction but this was lower in patients than in controls (56 ± 6% versus 63 ± 7%; mean ± SD), reflecting the presence of previous MI in a proportion of the patient group. The mean left ventricular ejection fraction fell during exercise in patients to 52 ± 15% and rose in controls to 74 ± 9%. Much of the discriminant value of the test lay in the exercise left ventricular ejection fraction alone, rather than in the change from rest to exercise.

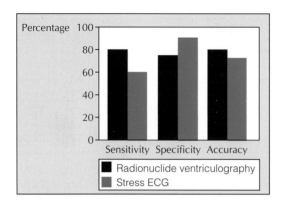

Fig. 3.11. *Comparison of sensitivity and specificity of stress ECG and radionuclide ventriculography.*

The sensitivity of the test was not related to the percentage of women in a study but the specificity was inversely related (r = –0.65, P < 0.001), that is, more false-positive tests occurred in women. Sensitivity was slightly higher in studies in which antianginal therapy was stopped before the test (87% versus 78%) (Fig. 3.11).

Gibson and Beller [20] compared thallium scanning and radionuclide ventriculography in 391 patients. The sensitivity and specificity for thallium scanning was 84% and 92% and for radionuclide ventriculography 85% and 79%. There is probably little to choose between the two when deciding which to use as a diagnostic test.

Stress echocardiography

Stress echocardiography has recently gained acceptance as a useful tool in the management of patients with CHD [50–55]. In experienced hands, it has a relatively low cost, good sensitivity and high specificity. It detects the onset of regional wall motion abnormalities, which are the first manifestations of the ischaemic cascade.

Physical exercise is the most natural way of testing coronary reserve but image optimization is often difficult. Supine bicycle ergometry is the usual mode of choice. Adenosine, dipyridamole and dobutamine are used in clinical practice to produce pharmacological stress. Adenosine causes marked vasodilatation in normal coronary vessels and dipyridamole achieves the same effect by inhibiting the breakdown of adenosine. Coronary perfusion is reduced by means of coronary steal, thus inducing myocardial ischaemia in the territory of diseased vessels. Dobutamine is a sympathomimetic amine able to increase myocardial contractility and oxygen consumption by directly stimulating alpha-1 and beta-1 cardiac receptors.

Marwick [56] reviewed studies between 1979 and 1993 comparing the various modes of stress echocardiography in the diagnosis of CHD (Fig. 3.12). The studies involved 1756 patients and 694 controls. The overall sensitivity of the three tests were comparable but specificity was highest for vasodilator echocardiography.

Echocardiography seems to retain a high specificity in women and may be particularly useful in those women with typical and atypical pain who fall into an intermediate probability of disease group [50,51]. Marwick *et al.* [50] compared exercise echocardiography with exercise ECG and found that exercise echocardiography had

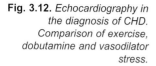

Fig. 3.12. *Echocardiography in the diagnosis of CHD. Comparison of exercise, dobutamine and vasodilator stress.*

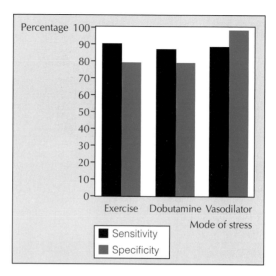

a higher specificity and accuracy, permitting a better stratification in patients, thus avoiding unnecessary angiography. Further studies are obviously required to clarify the place of each modality but these results are encouraging. The advantage that exercise echocardiography holds is in the great wealth of data relating to prognosis based on work capacity. This makes it the author's mode of choice, despite the lower accuracy reported by Gianrossi [36] (see Fig. 3.7).

The future — positron emission tomography?

Positron emission tomography (PET) is now accepted as the most accurate non-invasive method for the diagnosis of CHD. The average cost is approximately US$1800 per study, which includes running and replacement costs of equipment and doctor's fee. The reported sensitivity and specificity are around 95% [31] (Fig. 3.13).

Although we should expect a slight decline of both values in the future, as previously discussed, this has yet to be reported. Its superiority to other noninvasive tests remains to be proven. Compared with single photon emission computed tomography imaging, it offers better spatial resolution, higher count rate and better attenuation correction, allowing better detection of CHD and greater accuracy in the assessment of disease severity [66,67].

PET is now at the heart of a wide debate among cardiologists to determine its real place in the hierarchy of the noninvasive tests. The very high sensitivity and specificity place it as the 'noninvasive gold standard' of the 1990s, its more widespread use being limited mainly by its costs. However, it could effectively abolish the need for diagnostic coronary angiography, with angiography being restricted only to those who have a demonstrable need for revascularization. Much more evidence is required to show that PET can truly

Study	No. of patients	Sensitivity	Specificity
Derner [57]	193	94	95
Gupta [58]	48	94	95
Williams [59]	208	98	93
Go [60]	132	95	82
Gould [61]	50	95	100
Stewart [62]	81	85	88
Tamaki [63]	51	98	100
Schelbert [64]	32	97	100
Yonekura [65]	60	97	100
Total/average	**855**	**95**	**95**

Fig. 3.13. *Sensitivity and specificity of cardiac PET.*

determine the severity of coronary disease and in particular detect regression and progression during medical therapy [37,38], before this argument can be accepted.

Summary

Although a surprising suggestion at first, PET could become a highly cost-effective tool for the diagnosis of coronary artery disease, completely displacing the other noninvasive tests and reducing the need for angiography.

The diagnosis of CHD, as advocated here, may require the use of computers to replace the clinical or intuitive approach with that of a more evidence-based strategy [69,70]. The means to do this have been around for a long time [71] and will be one of the most powerful ways to argue for the allocation of more health-care resources [72].

References

1. Kupersmith J *et al.*: **Cost effectiveness analysis in heart disease, Part III: ischaemia, congestive heart failure, and arrhythmias.** *Prog Cardiovasc Dis* 1995, 37:307–346.

2. Brook RH: **Appropriateness: the next frontier.** *BMJ* 1994, 308:218–219.

3. Hampton JR: **Practice variations, appropriateness and decision analysis.** *QJM* 1995, 88:365–367.

4. Schoenbaum SC: **Toward fewer procedures and better outcomes.** *JAMA* 1993, 269:794–796.

5. Forfar JC, Firoozan S: **Application of coronary angiography in the UK: disease severity or physician** preference? *QJM* 1995, 88:147–148.

6. Yusuf S *et al.*: **Effect of coronary artery bypass graft surgery on survival: overview of 10-year results from randomised trials by the Coronary Artery Bypass Graft Surgery Trialists Collaboration.** *Lancet* 1994, 344:563–570.

7. Gray D *et al.*: **Audit of coronary angiography and bypass surgery.** *Lancet* 1990, 335:1317–1320.

8. Graboysa TB *et al.*: **Results of a second-opinion trial among patients recommended for coronary angiography.** *JAMA* 1992, 268:2537–2540.

9. Henderson RA *et al.*: **Variations in the use of**

coronary arteriography in the UK: the RITA trial coronary arteriogram register. *QJM* 1995, **88**:167–173.

10. Chassin MR *et al.*: **How coronary angiography is used. Clinical determinants of appropriateness.** *JAMA* 1987, **258**:2543–2547.

11. Bernstein SJ *et al.*: **The appropriateness of use of coronary angiography in New York State.** *JAMA* 1993, **269**:766–769.

12. Winslow CM *et al.*: **The appropriateness of performing coronary artery bypass surgery.** *JAMA* 1988, **260**:505–509.

13. Leape LL *et al.*: **The appropriateness of use of coronary artery bypass graft surgery in New York State.** *JAMA* 1993, **269**:753–760.

14. Kotler TS, Diamond GA: **Exercise thallium-201 scintigraphy in the diagnosis and prognosis of coronary artery disease.** *Ann Intern Med* 1990, **119**:684–702.

15. Ladenheim ML *et al.*: **Incremental prognostic power of clinical history, exercise electrocardiography and myocardial perfusion scintigraphy in suspected coronary artery disease.** *Am J Cardiol* 1987, **59**:270–277.

16. Hilborne LH *et al.*: **The appropriateous of use of percutaneous transluminal coronary angioplasty in New York State.** *JAMA* 1993, **269**:761–765.

17. Patterson RE *et al.*: **Comparison of modalities to diagnose coronary artery disease.** *Semin Nucl Med* 1994, **24**:286–310.

18. Diamond GA, Forrester JS: **Analysis of probability as an aid in the clinical diagnosis of coronary-artery disease.** *N Engl J Med* 1979, **300**:1350–1358.

19. Patterson RE, Horowitz SF: **Importance of epidemiology and biostatistics in deciding clinical strategies for using diagnostic tests: a simplified approach using examples from coronary artery disease.** *J Am Coll Cardiol* 1989, **13**:1653–1665.

20. Gibson RS, Beller GA: **Should exercise electrocardiographic testing be replaced by radioisotope methods.** In *Controversies in Coronary Artery Disease.* Edited by Rahimtoola SH. *Cardiovascular Clinics* **13/1**:1–32.

21. Weiner DA *et al.*: **Correlations among history of angina, ST-segment response and prevalence of coronary-artery disease in the Coronary Artery Surgery Study (CASS).** *N Engl J Med* 1979, **301**:230–235.

22. Northridge DB, Hall RJC: **Post-myocardial-infarction exercise testing in the thrombolytic era.** *Lancet* 1994, **343**:1175–1176.

23. Villela A *et al.*: **Prognostic significance of maximal exercise testing after myocardial infarction treated with thrombolytic agents: the GISSI-2 database.** *Lancet* 1995, **346**:523–529.

24. Hertzer NR *et al.*: **Coronary artery disease in peripheral vascular patients. A classification of 1000 coronary angiograms and results of surgical management.** *Ann Surg* 1984, **199**:223–233.

25. Pryor DV *et al.*: **Estimating the likelihood of significant coronary artery disease.** *Am J Med* 1983, **75**:771–780.

26. Weintraub WS *et al.*: **Critical analysis of the application of Bayes' theorem to sequential testing in the noninvasive diagnosis of coronary artery disease.** *Am J Cardiol* 1984, **54**:43–49.

27. Rembold CM, Watson D: **Post-test probability calculation by weights.** *Ann Intern Med* 1988, **108**:115–120.

28. Patterson RE *et al.*: **Practical diagnosis of coronary artery disease. A Bayes' theorem nomogram to correlate clinical data with noninvasive exercise tests.** *Am J Cardiol* 1984, **53**:252–256.

29. Diamond GA: **Reverend Bayes' silent majority: an alternative factor affecting sensitivity and specificity of exercise electrocardiography.** *Am J Cardiol* 1986, **57**:1175–1180.

30. Diamond GA *et al.*: **Prior restraint: a Bayesian perspective on the optimization of technology utilization for diagnosis of coronary artery disease.** *Am J Cardiol* 1995, **76**:82–86.

31. Patterson RE *et al.*: **Comparison of cost-effectiveness and utility of exercise ECG, single photon emission tomography, positron emission tomography, and coronary angiography for diagnosis of coronary artery disease.** *Circulation* 1995, **91**:54–65.

32. Rozanski A *et al.*: **The declining specificity of exercise radionuclide ventriculography.** *N Engl J Med* 1983, **309**:518–522.

33. Detrano R *et al.*: **The diagnostic accuracy of the exercise electrocardiogram. A meta-analysis of 22 years of research.** *Progress Cardiovasc Dis* 1989, **32**:173–206.

34. Detrano R *et al.*: **Exercise induced ST segment depression in the diagnosis of multivessel coronary disease. A meta-analysis.** *J Am Coll Cardiol* 1989, **14**:1501–1508.

35. Rozanski A, Berman DS: **The efficacy of cardiovascular nuclear medicine exercise studies.** *Semin Nucl Med* 1987, **17**:104–120.

36. Gianrossi R *et al.*: **Exercise induced ST depression in the diagnosis of coronary artery disease. A meta-analysis.** *Circulation* 1989, **80**:87–98.

37. Gould KL: **Reversal of coronary atherosclerosis: clinical promise as the basis for the non-invasive management of coronary artery disease.** *Circulation* 1994, **90**:1558–1571.

38. Gould KL *et al.*: **Non invasive management of coronary artery disease.** *Lancet* 1995, **346**:750–753.

39. Mark DB *et al.*: **Prognostic value of a treadmill exercise score in outpatients with suspected coronary artery disease.** *N Engl J Med* 1991, **325**:849–853.

40. Okin PM, Kligfield P: **Heart rate adjustment of ST segment depression and performance of the exercise electrocardiogram: a critical evaluation.** *J Am Coll Cardiol* 1995, **25**:1726–1735.

41. Kamata J *et al.*: **ST-segment/heart rate loop analysis on treadmill exercise testing can provide diagnostic and prognostic information in patients with stable effort angina.** *Coronary Artery Dis* 1995, **6**:547–554.

42. Detrano R *et al.*: **Exercise electrocardiographic**

variables: a critical appraisal. *J Am Coll Cardiol* 1986, 8:836–847.

43. Ascoop CAPC *et al.*: **Cardiac exercise testing. Indications, staff, equipment, conduct and procedures.** *Neth J Cardiol* 1989, 2:63–72.

44. McCarthy DM: **Stress electrocardiography in women.** *Int J Cardiol* 1984, 5:727–729.

45. Surawicz B, Fisch C: **The changing role of the exercise electrocardiogram as a diagnostic and prognostic test for chronic ischaemic heart disease.** *J Am Coll Cardiol* 1986, 8:1195–1210.

46. Allen WH: **Five year follow-up of maximal treadmill stress test in asymptomatic men and women.** *Circulation* 1980, 62:522–527.

47. Manga *et al.*: **Different prognostic value of exercise electrocardiogram in men and women.** *Circulation* 1979, 63:312–317.

48 Barolski SM *et al.*: **Differences in electrocardiographic response to exercise of women and men: a non-Bayesian factor.** *Circulation* 1979, 60:1021–1027.

49. Robert AR *et al.*: **Logistic discriminant analysis improves diagnostic accuracy of exercise testing for coronary artery disease in women.** *Circulation* 1991, 83:1202–1209.

50. Marwick TH *et al.*: **Exercise echocardiography is an accurate and cost-efficient technique for detection of coronary artery disease in women.** *J Am Coll Cardiol* 1995, 26:335–341.

51. Sawada SG *et al.*: **Exercise echocardiographic detection of coronary artery disease in women.** *J Am Coll Cardiol* 1989, 14:1440–1447.

52. Picano E, Lattanzi F: **Dipyridamole echocardiography. A new diagnostic window on coronary artery disease.** *Circulation* 1991, 83(suppl III): III-19–III-26.

53. Pirelli S *et al.*: **Exercise electrocardiography versus dipyridamole echocardiography testing in coronary angioplasty.** *Circulation* 1991, 83(suppl III): III-38–III-42.

54. Dagianti A *et al.*: **Stress echocardiography: comparison of exercise dipyridamole and dobutamine in detecting and predicting the extent of coronary artery disease.** *J Am Coll Cardiol* 1995, 26:18–25.

55. Johns JP *et al.*: **Dipyridamole-thallium versus dobutamine echocardiographic stress testing. A clinician's viewpoint.** *Am Heart J* 1995, **130**:373–385.

56. Marwick TA: **Stress echocardiography. Its role in the diagnosis and evaluation of coronary artery disease.** In *Stress Echocardiography.* USA: Kluwer Academic Publishers; 1994.

57. Demer LL *et al.*: **Assessment of coronary artery disease severity by positron emission tomography: comparison with quantitative arteriography.** *Circulation* 1989, 79:825.

58. Gupta NC *et al.*: **Adenosine in myocardial perfusion inaging using positron emission tomography.** *Am Heart J* 1992, **12**:293–301.

59. Williams. *J Myocardial Ischaemia* 1990, **2**:38 (Both the publisher and the author have been unable to find full details for this reference.)

60. Go RT: **A prospective comparison of rubidium-82 PET and thallium-201 SPECT myocardial perfusion imaging utilizing a single dipyridamole stress in the diagnosis of coronary artery disease.** *J Nucl Med* 1990, **31**:1899–1905.

61. Gould KL *et al.*: **Non invasive assessment of coronary stenosis by myocardial perfusion imaging during pharmacologic coronary vasodilation. VIII. Clinical feasability of positron imaging without a cyclotron using a generator produced rubidium-82.** *J Am Coll Cardiol* 1986, 7:775–789.

62. Stewart RE *et al.*: **Comparison of rubidium-82 positron emission tomography and thallium-201 SPECT imaging for detection of coronary artery disease.** *Am J Cardiol* 1991, **67**:1303–1310.

63. Tamaki N: **Value and limitation of stress thallium-201 single photon emission computed tomography: comparison with nitrogen-13 ammonia positron tomography.** *J Nucl Med* 1988, 29:1181–1188.

64. Schlebert HR *et al.*: **Non-invasive assessment of coronary stenosis by myocardial imaging during pharmacologic coronary vasodilation. VI: detection of coronary artery disease in human beings with intravenous N-13 ammonia and positron computed tomography.** *Am J Cardiol* 1982, 49:1197–1207.

65. Yonekura Y *et al.*: **Detection of coronary artery disease with ^{13}N-ammonia and high-resolution positron-emission computed tomography.** *Am Heart J* 1987, **113**:645–665.

66. Garcia EV *et al.*: **What should we expect from cardiac PET?** *J Nucl Med* 1993, 34:978–980.

67. Gould KL: **PET perfusion imaging and nuclear cardiology.** *J Nucl Med* 1991, **32**:579–606.

68. Lewin B *et al.*: **The angina management programme. Rehabilitation treatment.** *Br J Cardiol* 1995, 2:193–198.

69. Diamond GA *et al.*: **Clinician decisions and computers.** *J Am Coll Cardiol* 1987, 9:1385–1396.

70. Melin JA *et al.*: **Alternative diagnostic strategies for coronary artery disease in women: demonstration of the usefulness and efficiency of probability analysis.** *Cardiology* 1985, 71:535–542.

71. Diamond GA *et al.*: **Computer-assisted diagnosis in the noninvasive evaluation of patients with suspected coronary artery disease.** *J Am Coll Cardiol* 1983, 1:444–445.

72. Kellett J, Graham J: **Referral for coronary angiography after exercise testing: traditional decision-making versus decision analysis.** *QJM* 1995, **88**:401–408.

Risk stratification in coronary heart disease
John McMurray

Introduction

The purpose of risk stratification

Risk stratification in angina pectoris aims to identify those patients at greatest risk of an adverse event, principally death or nonfatal MI. However, the value of such a process is limited unless the high-risk patients identified can be offered treatment that will improve their prognosis. In practice, this means identifying patients who might benefit from CABG. With expensive treatments such as CABG, which have significant morbidity and mortality, it is hoped that risk stratification will identify the small proportion of the population in whom most of the risk of adverse events and benefit of treatment is concentrated.

Natural history studies

Trials carried out at large centres attract certain types of patient, so referrals may not be truly representative of the general population and predictions based on such populations may have less value in other populations. In many studies, the highest-risk patients have been excluded because treatment was indicated or because the patient was too unwell to undergo investigations such as exercise testing. Patients may undergo CABG or PTCA during the course of follow-up. Such procedures remove particularly high-risk patients from the study population. There is no satisfactory way of dealing with such 'drop outs' and the natural history studies predating the widespread use of CABG are, consequently, of particular value (although modern medical therapy may also have improved prognosis). Conversely the need for CABG or PTCA is treated as an adverse event in some studies, although the decision to undertake these procedures may be influenced by certain test results, thus increasing its predictive value.

Patient history and other clinical characteristics

Age and sex

Older patients have a worse prognosis; in part this may be due to an increase in coronary artery disease with advancing age [1]. Women, especially younger women, have a better prognosis than men with angina (although this is not the case after MI) [2,3]. This difference may be explained, at least in part, by the fact that more women have 'normal' coronary arteries at angiography.

Intensity of angina and angina scores

The Duke University database [4] contains data on 5886 patients who underwent cardiac catheterization between 1969 and 1984. Analysis of the data showed that the frequency and tempo of symptoms were of important predictive value. Combination of the results with analysis of the resting 12-lead ECG, derived an 'angina score'.

Angina score = course [0–3] x (1 + ST-T abnormalities [0–6])

Range 0–24

At 0, patients had stable angina and no ST-T wave changes at rest

At 24, patients had unstable angina, five or more episodes of pain per day and ST-T wave changes at rest

---

The angina score added independent prognostic information to that found at cardiac catheterization. For example, patients with three-vessel disease and normal left ventricular function had a 2-year infarction-free survival of 90% if they had an angina score of 0 and 68% if they had an angina score of greater than 9.

Heart failure, digoxin and diuretic use

Several studies report an increased risk in patients with clinical evidence of heart failure. These findings are consistent with the evidence that previous MI, cardiomegaly on chest radiogaphy and impaired left ventricular function are strong predictors of poor subsequent outcome.

In the Mayo Clinic series [5], 5-year survival in 371 patients with heart failure was 20%, compared with 58% in the overall study population of 6882 patients. The University of Alabama study [6] showed a 22-month survival rate of 60% in 45 patients with heart failure, compared with a rate of 92% in the 201 patients without heart failure. The adverse prognostic effect of heart failure was present in patients with one-, two- or three-vessel coronary disease.

Medically treated patients in the CASS registry [3] with no or minimal heart failure had a 4-year survival rate of 90%, whereas those with moderate and severe heart failure had survival rates of 62% and 18%, respectively. Of the 25 clinical and exercise variables analysed in the 24 959 patients recruited, the presence of heart failure on examination was the single most powerful multivariate predictor of adverse outcome (Fig. 4.1) [3].

Hypertension

Concomitant hypertension worsens prognosis in patients with angina. In the Mayo Clinic series [5], 5-year survival in patients without hypertension was 63%. In patients with increasingly severe hypertension, categorized into Groups 1–4, 5-year survival was 63, 61, 46 and 22%, respectively. The New York Health Insurance Plan (HIP) study [7] investigated men aged 25–64 years with angina and is one of the most important

Fig. 4.1. *Significant predictors of survival by multivariate analysis in the CASS registry. *Large number indicates more powerful multivariate predictor.*

Covariate	Chi-square*
Clinical and exercise variables	
Congestive heart failure score	151
Previous MI	37
Final exercise test stage	30
Sex	30
Age	15
Cardiac enlargement	11
History of heart failure	8
ST-segment response during exercise	6
Clinical, exercise and angiographic variables	
Left ventricular score	201
Number of vessels affected	52
Congestive heart failure score	34
Final exercise stage	16
Cardiac enlargement	6
Sex	5

unselected natural history studies. Here, a causal entry blood pressure of greater than 160 mmHg systolic or 95 mmHg diastolic was associated with a 30-month mortality of 18.6%, compared with 7.8% in people with normal blood pressure.

Other clinical predictors of risk

Smoking, obesity, inactivity, diabetes and peripheral vascular disease are also associated with a worse outcome in patients with angina [5,8–10].

Simple investigations

12-lead ECG

The resting 12-lead ECG adds valuable incremental prognostic information to the clinical history and examination. In the New York HIP study [7], 30-month mortality was 21% in men with a specific resting ECG abnormality (usually > 0.5 mm ST-segment depression), compared with 5% in those with a normal ECG.

The resting 'ischaemic' ECG ST–T-wave changes are a powerful independent predictor of prognosis, adding to information obtained from the clinical history [4]. Combined with historical information, ST–T abnormalities on the ECG allowed derivation of an angina score that defined a high-risk group of patients. This score gave incremental information to that provided by cardiac catheterization (although cardiac catheterization also added predictive information to the angina score).

45

T-wave inversion in leads V1 and V2 is associated with a 5-year survival of 29% compared with 73% in patients with a normal ECG [5]. Left bundle branch block also indicated a grave prognosis in patients with angina, with a 5-year survival of 37%.

ECG evidence of established Q-wave MI in patients with angina is associated with an increased risk of premature death. The 24% of patients with this ECG abnormality had a 22-month mortality of 31%, compared with 7% in those with a normal ECG, regardless of the number of diseased vessels.

Recent evidence from the Icelandic Heart Association Preventative Clinic study [11] of 9141 men, aged 53–80 years, suggests that an old unrecognised infarct in patients with angina identifies a particularly high-risk group.

ECG and clinical left ventricular hypertrophy are associated with a reduced survival rate [11,12]. Premature ventricular beats also may suggest poor outcome, although these may be simply markers of impaired left ventricular function [9]. Clinical and ECG risk factors interact. In the New York HIP study [7], men with both hypertension and ECG abnormalities had a 30-month mortality of 32%, compared with 3.5% in people with normal blood pressure and a normal ECG. The high-risk subgroup constituted 11% of the total cohort of 275 patients.

Chest radiography

Cardiomegaly, suggesting the presence of impaired left ventricular function or left ventricular hypertrophy is also associated with a poor clinical outcome [13]. In the University of Alabama study [6], 118 patients with increased heart volume had a 22-month mortality of 23%, compared with only 3% in 93 men with normal heart volume.

Importance of history, examination and simple investigations

Clinical history, examination and simple investigations provide valuable prognostic information. The single most predictive finding is diagnosis of heart failure, which was found in 5–18% of patients in the angina studies [5,6].

An older man with heart failure, ECG evidence of Q-wave infarction, cardiomegaly on chest radiography and increasing frequency of angina is clearly at high risk. Further investigation is unlikely to add useful predictive information in this individual and such people have often been excluded from the more recent studies investigating the role of particular specialist investigations.

Special investigations: noninvasive tests

Many good reviews of investigations in risk stratifying patients have been published [8,14–23].

Exercise ECG

Not performing an exercise test is associated with a poor outcome [8], probably because patients in this category are older and hence more likely to have heart failure or peripheral vascular disease, both of which adversely affect prognosis. The exercise test variables found to have important prognostic significance are shown in Figure 4.2.

Fig. 4.2. *Exercise test predictors of prognosis.*

Inability to undertake exercise test

Exercise time

Degree of ST-segment depression

Blood pressure response to exercise

Ventricular arrhythmias during exercise

Maximum heart rate achieved

The CASS registry [3,24] contains one of the largest bodies of data on exercise testing in patients with CHD. The final stage of exercise achieved and the degree of ST-segment depression enabled a distinction to be made between subgroups with a five-fold difference in annual mortality (Fig. 4.3). Patients without ischaemia (< 1 mm ST-segment depression) and a good exercise tolerance (final stage higher than Stage III of the standard Bruce protocol) had an annual mortality of less than 1% over 4 years. This constituted 34% of the total of 4083 patients studied. Patients with a poor exercise tolerance (lower than Stage I) and greater ST-segment depression (> 1 mm) had an annual mortality of more than 5%. Exercise tolerance was more important than ischaemia in determining prognosis. Patients with greater than 1 mm ST-segment depression still had a good prognosis (2% annual mortality) if they managed to achieve Stage III of the Bruce protocol on exercise testing.

Another study [25] showed that 5-year survival in patients who developed greater than 2 mm ST-segment depression during exercise varied from 100% in those who reached Stage IV of the Bruce Protocol to 52% in those who were unable to complete Stage I. Although exercise duration was a strong indictor of prognosis it did not predict the risk of nonfatal events, at least among those patients with more than 2 mm ST-segment depression who were studied. The study also suggested that angiography was unhelpful in predicting the risk of unstable angina or MI [26]. The latest 16-year follow-up of CASS registry patients confirms that exercise tolerance time is the most important of all clinical and exercise variables [24]. Exercise testing adds incremental prognostic information to the clinical history and examination, a finding substantiated in several studies. Preliminary evidence suggests that tests on treatment may be more predictive of multivessel disease and recurrent ischaemia [27] but this remains to be proved.

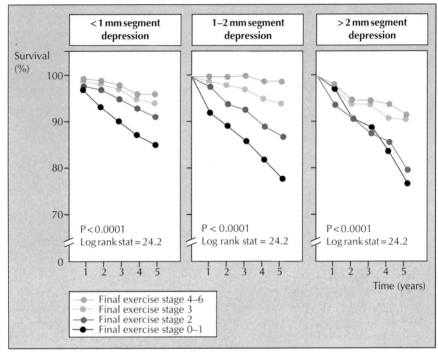

Fig. 4.3. *Prognostic importance of an ECG profile and exercise test in medically treated patients with coronary artery disease. Cumulative survival rates based on the final exercise stage achieved for patients with < 1 mm, 1–2 mm and > 2 mm ST-segment depression during exercise testing. Adapted with permission from Weiner et al. [3].*

Combined clinical and exercise test prognostic scoring systems

Two studies have recently combined clinical and exercise variables into risk categories to allow further stratification of patients with CHD [14,28–31].

The Long Beach Veterans Administration Medical Centre Group derived a score based on the presence of one clinical variable (heart failure) and three exercise test responses (mm of ST-segment depression, change in systolic blood pressure, exercise capacity in metabolic equivalents [METs]) to classify patients into low-, intermediate- and high-risk categories [11,14,28,29].

Angina score = 5(CHF/digoxin) + (mm exercise-induced ST-segment depression) + change in SBP score – METs

CHF, congestive heart failure; SBP, systolic blood pressure; METs, metabolic equivalents

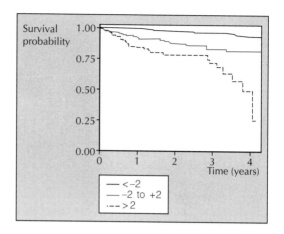

Fig 4.4. *Kaplan–Meier plots of average cardiovascular mortality for ranges of the Long Beach Veterans Administration Medical Centre prognostic score. Adapted with permission from Morrow et al. [28].*

The annual mortality in these categories were 2, 7 and 15%, respectively (Fig. 4.4). A score of less than –2 was associated with an annual cardiovascular mortality of less than 2%. The Veterans Administration found that 53% of patients undergoing cardiac catheterization and 35% of those undergoing CABG had a prognostic score of less than –2 [14].

The Duke University group derived a scoring system using three treadmill variables, exercise tolerance in METs, mm ST-segment depression and presence or absence of angina on treadmill (Fig.4.5) [14,30–32].

Angina score = METs –5 (mm exercise-induced ST-segment
depression) – 4 (treadmill angina index)

Again low-, intermediate- and high-risk groups were identified among inpatients with angina [30]. Five-year mortality was 3, 9 and 28%, respectively. This scoring system accurately predicted prognosis in an unselected outpatient population (see Fig. 4.5) [32]. In the outpatient validation study, 62% of patients were categorized as low-risk (99% 5-year survival), 34% as intermediate-risk (95% 5-year survival) and 4% as high-risk (79% 5-year survival). The treadmill score added significantly to the prognostic information obtained from clinical findings. However, many higher-risk patients, including the elderly and those with severe left ventricular dysfunction and heart failure, did not participate in many of these large exercise studies. As such, exercise testing is likely to add prognostic information only in low-risk patients.

Ambulatory ECG monitoring

Approximately 50% of patients with angina and stabilized coronary artery disease show usually transient episodes of ST-segment depression and as many as 75% of all ischaemic episodes may be 'silent' [33–36]. In these patients ambulatory ECG ST-segment

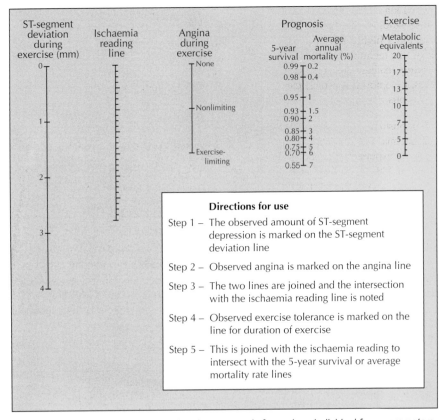

Fig 4.5. *The Duke nomogram for estimating prognosis for a given individual from parameters of Duke score. Adapted with permission from Marks* et al. *[31].*

depression seems to indicate a worse prognosis, although the predictive value of this finding may be greatest in patients with more severe coronary disease. Whether ambulatory ECG ST-segment depression gives prognostic information over and above that obtained from exercise testing is much less clear. There is some evidence that in patients with a positive exercise test, ambulatory ECG ST-segment depression gives incremental prognostic information, although 'outcome' in these studies did include the 'soft' endpoint of need for revascularization. The incremental value of ambulatory ECG monitoring compared with other investigations has not been fully established. The US National Institutes of Health [36] are investigating whether suppression of silent ischaemic episodes improves prognosis.

Radionuclide myocardial perfusion imaging: thallium-201

The use of radionuclide myocardial perfusion imaging has recently been reviewed in detail [21,37,38]. Compared with exercise ECG testing, there have been relatively fewer long-term follow-up studies involving large numbers of unselected patients. Those studies that have been reported come from centres of excellence, usually studying a highly selected population, raising concerns about the wider applicability of this technique.

Stress thallium-201 scintigraphy [21,37,38] is the most widely studied technique. The stressor employed is usually exercise, although pharmacological agents have been used.

Various information can be obtained from thallium scanning:

• Demonstration of reversible myocardial perfusion deficits, considered to represent ischaemia. The number and severity of the deficits give prognostic information, showing an exponential relationship between risk and the number of reversible thallium defects [38]. A number of studies consistently confirm the very good prognosis of patients with a normal thallium scan [21].

• Demonstration of irreversible myocardial perfusion deficits, considered to represent infarction. Recent reports have indicated that late redistribution often occurs [39].

• Demonstration of increased lung uptake of thallium. This is secondary to pulmonary congestion. The lung–heart ratio of thallium uptake is a particularly powerful predictor of risk. The cardiac event rate at 5 years was 5% in 192 patients with a normal thallium scan, 25% in 163 patients with an abnormal thallium myocardial perfusion scan but normal lung activity and 67% in the 81 patients with increased lung uptake of thallium [40].

• Demonstration of transient left ventricular cavity dilatation, thought to represent ischaemic left ventricular dysfunction [41].

Although there is little doubt that thallium-201 myocardial perfusion imaging does give prognostic information, the real question is whether it adds incremental information to that obtained from clinical findings and exercise ECG testing.

In experienced hands, exercise thallium-201 myocardial perfusion imaging does add to the predictive information gained from clinical data and exercise ECG [42]. However, the greatest incremental predictive information obtained is that left ventricular dysfunction is of major prognostic significance, information that could have been obtained more easily by echocardiography.

Dipyridamole thallium imaging also gives prognostic information but its value compared with other noninvasive tests remains to be determined [21]. Limited data from studies using newer myocardial perfusion tracers such as technetium-99m sestamibi suggests that these agents also provide prognostic information in patients with CHD.

Radionuclide ventriculography

Measurement of left ventricular function at rest and during exercise is thought to provide information on the extent of irreversible and reversible myocardial damage and its role in risk stratification has been recently reviewed [23]. Increasing evidence that viable myocardium may be noncontractile ('hibernating') indicates that this older view may be too simplistic. There is no doubt, however, that resting left ventricular function is of great prognostic importance. Failure of ejection fraction to rise appropriately on exercise predicts a poor outcome. For example, in over 100 patients with a resting ejection fraction of more than 30%, a fall in ejection fraction of 10% or more identified a group of medically treated patients with an annual mortality risk of approximately 6% [22]. This risk was 12 times that of patients with a fall in ejection fraction of less than 5% on exercise. Ejection fraction response to exercise can also add incremental prognostic information to that obtained from exercise ECG testing alone (Fig 4.6) [43].

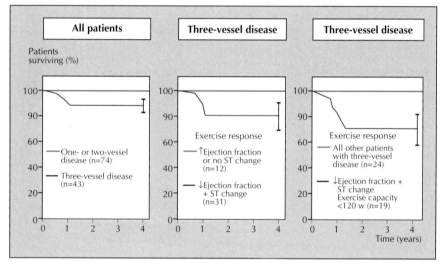

Fig. 4.6. *The relationship between ejection fraction and prognosis-exercise response. Adapted with permission from Bonow et al. [43].*

Echocardiography

Echocardiography is more widely available, cheaper and quicker to perform than radionuclide ventriculography and does not involve exposure to radiation. However, it has disadvantages. Not all patients provide high-quality echocardiographic images and precise measurement of global and regional contractile function, especially during and after exercise, is technically demanding.

Surprisingly little information is available on the prognostic potential of echocardiographically measured resting left ventricular function in patients with angina, although there is no reason to believe that it should be any less useful than radionuclide ventriculography or cardiac catheterization.

The role of both exercise and pharmacological stress echocardiography in prognostic stratification of patients with CHD has been under intense investigation [44–46]. Most available information relates to risk stratification of MI survivors rather than patients with angina. The preliminary data suggest that, in expert hands, stress echocardiography is of predictive value in CHD.

Cardiac catheterization: coronary anatomy

Several major studies describe the prognostic significance of coronary artery obstruction, whereby the greater the extent of coronary arterial narrowing, the worse the outcome. The most interesting of these reports come from Johns Hopkins University and the University of Alabama [6,47]. Although small, these studies are of great importance because they predate the widespread introduction of CABG but they have been overshadowed by the much larger series collected in trials of CABG, in particular the CASS registry [48,49].

The CASS registry reported on more than 20 000 medically treated patients, of whom 73% had exertional angina, 12% had angina at rest and 48% had a history of MI. Survival was related to the number, site (proximal or distal) and vessel stenosed. Survival in patients with one-, two- and three-vessel disease is shown in Figure 4.7. Mortality increases significantly as the extent of coronary disease increases.

Fig. 4.7. *Survival for medically treated CASS patients by number of diseased vessels, with three categories for zero-vessel disease: normal, minimal, and moderate. Adapted with permission from Edmond et al. [49].*

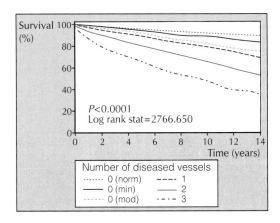

Patients with left main coronary artery disease had a particularly bad prognosis, a finding confirmed in other studies [50]. Five-year survival in patients with left main stenosis was only 48%. Left main equivalent, combined proximal circumflex and left anterior descending stenoses, were also associated with a poor prognosis (5-year survival 54%) [48]. Stenosis of the left anterior descending artery, proximal to its first septal branch, has also been associated with a poor outcome [51]. However, in patients without severe symptoms or signs of ischaemia induced by exercise, left main coronary disease may not carry such an unfavourable prognosis [52,53].

In the CASS registry [54], the 5-year survival of patients with proximal narrowings of one, two or three vessels was 77, 58 and 40% respectively. Comparable survival rates in those with nonproximal narrowings were 88, 74 and 56%.

Despite the emphasis placed on the prognostic importance of 'significant' stenoses (stenoses > 70% of the internal vessel diameter), other stenoses may also be of value. Early angiographic studies considered a reduction in internal vessel diameter of more

53

than 50% (i.e. a reduction in cross-sectional area of > 75%) to be 'significant' and found these measurements to be predictive of outcome in much the same way as the later studies that used the more than 70% criterion [6,47]. Recent evidence from patients undergoing serial angiography suggests that often a 'nonsignificant' stenosis, rather than a 'significant' one, leads to infarction [55]. Although severe stenoses may be individually more likely to progress to complete occlusion, there are numerically more 'minor' stenoses and occlusion may be more likely to occur at the site of a minor lesion.

Left ventricular function

In the CASS registry, ejection fraction was of more prognostic importance than the number of coronary vessels stenosed (Fig. 4.8) [6,48,49]. Patients with one-vessel disease but an ejection fraction of less than 35% had a 4-year survival rate of 72%, whereas patients with three-vessel disease and an ejection fraction of more than 50% had a 4-year survival rate of 82%. Similar outcomes were seen if regional wall motion scores were used instead of ejection fraction.

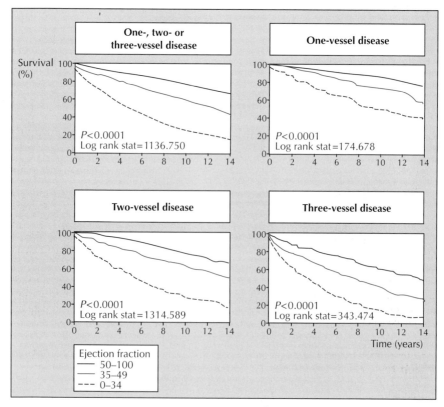

Fig. 4.8. *Survival for medically treated CASS patients with one-, two- or three-vessel disease by ejection fraction. Adapted with permission from Edmond et al. [49].*

Although left ventricular function and the number of coronary vessels stenosed are powerful predictors of prognosis, clinical variables add independent prognostic information. For example, in a recent study, patients with three-vessel disease, a left ventricular ejection fraction of less than 50% and a Duke angina score of 0 had a 5-year infarction-free survival rate of 76%, whereas those with an angina score of more than 9 had a survival rate of 56% [4]. In the CASS registry [56], 5-year survival for patients with three-vessel disease and impaired left ventricular function varied from 82 to 52% depending on the severity of angina.

Exercise-induced ischaemia, symptomatic or asymptomatic, adds prognostic information (see Fig. 4.6). Exercise time also adds important prognostic information, especially in patients with three-vessel disease and preserved ventricular function, a group of patients in whom the choice between medical and surgical treatment is perhaps most difficult (Fig. 4.9) [42].

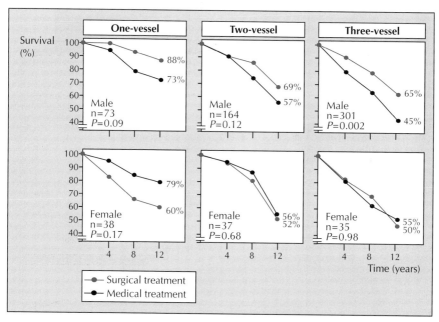

Fig. 4.9. *Cumulative survival rates for medically and surgically treated men and women, with high-risk exercise test and one-, two-, and three-vessel disease. Adapted with permission from Weiner et al. [24].*

Which tests are best?

The additive prognostic value of investigations carried out in a hierarchical order have been assessed, the 'tests' evaluated being clinical assessment, exercise thallium-201 perfusion imaging and cardiac catheterization [41]. Exercise testing added significantly to clinical assessment in the University of Virginia study [42] (Fig. 4.10).

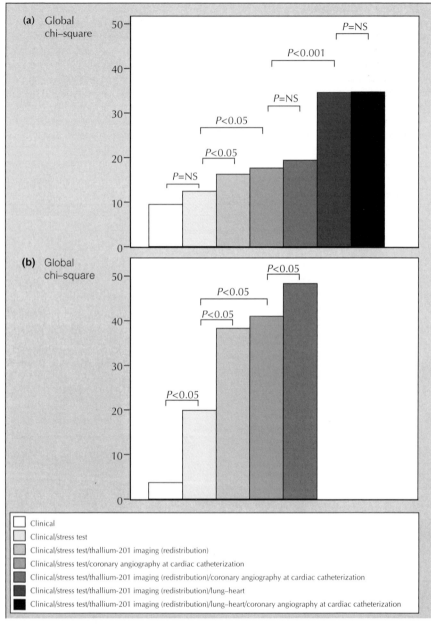

Fig. 4.10. *The incremental prognostic value (Chi-square value) of tests performed at (a) Massachusetts General Hospital and (b) University of Virginia. Adapted with permission from Pollock* et al. *[42].*

There and at the Massachusetts General Hospital, thallium perfusion imaging and cardiac catheterization added significantly to the prognostic information obtained from combined clinical examination and exercise testing. The incremental value from cardiac catheterization was no greater (and possibly less) than that of thallium perfusion imaging, but only coronary angiography was considered. The lung–heart thallium ratio was also calculated in the Massachusetts study. This added significantly more incremental prognostic information than coronary angiography or thallium perfusion imaging to that obtained from clinical and exercise stress evaluation. Therefore, coronary and ventricular angiography would probably be significantly better than coronary angiography alone and at least as good as the lung–heart thallium ratio estimate for risk stratification.

However, more information is required. For example, would another measure of left ventricular function give equivalent, incremental, prognostic information? Because the lung–heart thallium ratio added significantly more prognostic information than coronary angiography (and coronary angiography added nothing to the lung–heart ratio), might a measurement of resting left ventricular function be of as much incremental prognostic value as left ventricular and coronary angiography? The answer is probably yes, although this has yet to be formally evaluated.

Are the patients at risk the ones who benefit from surgery?

Although risk stratification can identify high-risk patients, whether these individuals would obtain a survival benefit from bypass surgery is not clear. Survival benefit has been most closely related to coronary anatomy and left ventricular function. However, exercise testing and other noninvasive investigations are not particularly predictive for multivessel coronary disease [23,57]. Consequently, there is a paradox in that noninvasive testing is accurate at predicting risk but not at identifying angiographic subsets of patients believed to obtain prognostic benefit from surgery. Also, high-risk patients with a left ventricular ejection fraction of less than 0.35 were excluded from the European CABG trial and the CASS randomized trial.

Several nonrandomized studies and retrospective analyses have suggested that high-risk patients may be better treated surgically [3,24]. Nonrandomized patients in the CASS registry who underwent exercise testing were divided into three groups according to risk: high (> 1 mm ST-segment depression, final stage of Bruce protocol < 1); medium (> 1 mm ST-segment depression, final stage > 1, or no ST-segment depression, final stage < 2); and low (no ST-segment depression, final stage > 3). Men and women in these groups with more than one operable vessel were compared with those treated surgically. Men in the high-risk group (but not the medium and low risk groups) treated surgically fared better (see Fig. 4.9). Twelve-year survival in medically treated patients was 55%, compared with a 69% survival rate in those treated surgically ($P = 0.0025$). The beneficial effects of surgery were seen mainly in men with three-vessel disease. No benefit of surgery was seen in women.

Whereas the highest-risk patients can be identified clinically, noninvasive and invasive investigations give important predictive information in other patients.

Risk stratification and unstable angina

An increase in the frequency or severity of angina, especially if accompanied by resting ECG changes, heralds a high risk of MI and death [58–60]. Patients are at greatest risk initially, but this decreases as angina stabilizes: those who do not stabilize with medical treatment have a particularly bad prognosis [58]. A recent report showed that patients with a persistently high C-reactive protein (or serum amyloid A protein) concentration are at high risk of an adverse outcome [61]. Similarly, asymptomatic ST-segment shift on Holter monitoring during the acute phase of unstable angina seems to be predictive of early adverse outcome but may be less predictive of longer-term prognosis [58, 62]. Coronary stenosis morphology may also be predictive of adverse outcome and CABG improves prognosis in patients with three-vessel disease and in those with impaired left ventricular function [63,64].

In stabilized low- and intermediate-risk patients, risk stratification can be approached in the same way as in stable angina pectoris [58,59]. The AHCPR guidelines [59] suggest that exercise testing is a generally useful risk stratification tool for stabilized patients but indicate that timing of the investigations is of vital importance. They refer to a recent study that compared symptom-limited exercise testing performed 3–7 days after an episode of unstable angina and before hospital discharge with testing performed 1 month later [65]. The prognostic value of both tests was similar but the earlier test identified adverse events occurring in the first month after discharge, which represented half of the events occurring in the first year after admission. Thus, early testing is indicated to obtain maximum prognostic information.

Risk stratification and asymptomatic coronary artery disease

Asymptomatic coronary artery disease occurs frequently. Little, if anything, is known about the natural history of people with asymptomatic coronary disease and no evidence of MI. Several studies have described patients with exercise ECG or ambulatory ECG evidence of presumed myocardial ischaemia. About 5–10% of middle-aged men have such findings, the prevalence increasing with age and presence of coronary risk factors. Exercise-induced ST-segment depression is associated with a worse prognosis [66]. Several 'classic' studies have been made in this area, for example the Lipid Research Clinics Mortality Follow-up study (Fig. 4.11) [67]. In the Baltimore Longitudinal Study on Angina, asymptomatic ischaemia was predictive of a worse outcome independent of conventional risk factors such as smoking, blood pressure and cholesterol [68]. The 'Men Born in 1914' study [69] provides similar data for ambulatory ECG monitoring (Fig. 4.12). Overall, asymptomatic ischaemia seems to increase the risk of fatal and nonfatal coronary events approximately three- to four-fold. However, most coronary events still occur in the much larger population with a normal test.

This raises some important questions. Does treating asymptomatic ischaemia improve prognosis? If so, should we screen for asymptomatic ischaemia? The answer to the first question is that we do not know and, consequently, to the second, no. We still do not know for certain whether treating asymptomatic ischaemia in patients with declared coronary disease improves prognosis.

Fig. 4.11. *Cumulative mortality in asymptomatic men with initially strong positive (> 2 mm ST-segment depression), weak positive (> 1 mm ST-segment depression) and negative exercise treadmill results in the Lipid Research Clinics Primary Prevention trial in the placebo-treated arm. ETT, exercise tolerance test. Adapted with permission from Ekelund et al. [67].*

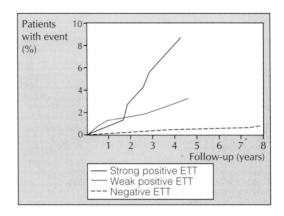

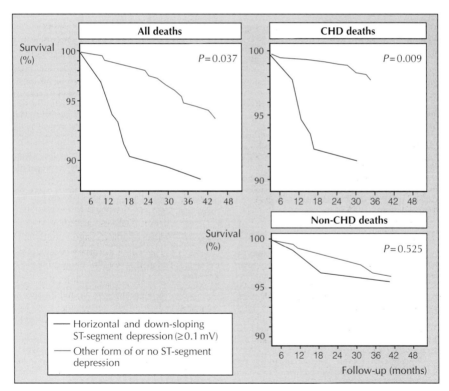

Fig 4.12. *Survival curves from the 'Men Born in 1914' study for men with horizontal or downsloping ST-segment depression on 24-h Holter monitoring and those with all other types of or no ST-segment depression. Adapted with permission from Hedblad et al. [69].*

References

1. Sigler LH: **Prognosis of angina pectoris and coronary occlusion.** *JAMA* 1951, **146**:998–1004.

2. Kannel WB, Feinleib M: **Natural history of angina pectoris in the Framingham Study.** *Am J Cardiol* 1972, **29**:154–163.

3. Weiner DA *et al.*: **Prognostic importance of a clinical profile and exercise test in medically treated patients with coronary artery disease.** *J Am Coll Cardiol* 1984, **3**:772–779.

4. Califf RM *et al.*: **Importance of clinical measures of ischaemia in the prognosis of patients with documented coronary artery disease.** *J Am Coll Cardiol* 1988, **11**:20–26.

5. Block WJ *et al.*: **Prognosis of angina pectoris observations in 6882 cases.** *JAMA* 1952, **150**:259–264.

6. Reeves TJ *et al.*: **Natural history of angina pectoris.** *Am J Cardiol* 1974, **33**:423–430.

7. Weinblatt E *et al.*: **Prognostic factors in angina pectoris: a prospective study.** *J Chron Dis* 1968, **21**: 231–245.

8. Friesinger GC: **The natural history of atherosclerotic coronary heart disease.** In *The Heart, arteries and veins (Hurst's The Heart)*, 8th edn. Edited by Hurst JW. McGraw-Hill; 1994:1185–1203.

9. Harris PJ *et al.*: **Survival in medically treated coronary artery disease.** *Circulation* 1979, **60**:1259–1269.

10. Sigurdsson E *et al.*: **Unrecognised myocardial infarction: epidemiology, clinical characteristics and prognostic role of angina pectoris.** *Ann Intern Med* 1995, **122**:96–102.

11. Morris K *et al.*: **Prediction of cardiovascular death by means of clinical and exercise test variables in patients selected for cardiac catheterisation.** *Am Heart J* 1993, **125**:1717–1726.

12. Hammermeister KE *et al.*: **Variables predictive of survival in patients with coronary disease.** *Circulation* 1979, **59**:421–430.

13. Bruce RA *et al.*: **Non-invasive predictors of sudden cardiac death in men with coronary heart disease.** *Am J Cardiol* 1977, **39**:833–840.

14. Chang JA, Froelicher VF: **Clinical and exercise test markers of prognosis in patients with stable coronary artery disease.** *Curr Probl Cardiol* 1994, **19**:533–587.

15. Silverman KJ, Grossman W: **Angina pectoris. Natural history and strategies for evaluation and management.** *N Eng J Med* 1984, **310**:1712–1717.

16. Helfant RH: **Stable angina pectoris: risk stratification and therapeutic options.** *Circulation* 1990, **82(suppl II)**:66–70.

17. Corne RA: **Risk stratification in stable angina pectoris.** *Am J Cardiol* 1987, **59**:695–697.

18. Weiner DA: **Risk stratification in angina pectoris.** *Cardiol Clin* 1991, **9**:39–47.

19. Hilton TC, Chaitman BR: **The prognosis in stable and unstable angina.** *Cardiol Clin* 1991, **9**:27–38.

20. Younis LT, Chaitman BR: **The prognostic value of exercise testing.** *Cardiol Clin* 1993, **11**:229–240.

21. Heller GV, Bown KA: **Prognosis of acute and chronic coronary artery disease by myocardial perfusion imaging.** *Cardiol Clin* 1994, **12**:271–287.

22. Borer JS *et al.*: **Assessment of coronary artery disease by radionuclide cineangiography.** *Cardiol Clin* 1994, **12**:333–357.

23. Bodenheimer MM: **Risk stratification in coronary disease: a contrary viewpoint.** *Ann Intern Med* 1992, **116**:927–936.

24. Weiner DA *et al.*: **Long-term prognostic value of exercise testing in men and women from the coronary artery surgery study (CASS) registry.** *Am J Cardiol* 1995, **75**:865–870.

25. Dagenais GR *et al.*: **Survival of patients with a strongly positive exercise electrocardiogram.** *Circulation* 1982, **65**:452–456.

26. Bogaty P *et al.*: **Prognosis in patients with a strongly positive electrocardiogram.** *Am J Cardiol* 1989, **64**:1284–1288.

27. Lim R *et al.*: **Exercise testing without interruption of medication for refining the selection of mildly symptomatic patients for prognostic coronary angiography.** *Br Heart J* 1994, **71**:334–340.

28. Morrow K *et al.*: **Prediction of cardiovascular death in men undergoing non-invasive evaluation for coronary artery disease.** *Ann Intern Med* 1993, **118**:689–695.

29. Froelicher V *et al.*: **Prediction of atherosclerotic cardiovascular death in men using a prognostic score.** *Am J Cardiol* 1994, **73**:133–138.

30. Marks DB *et al.*: **Exercise treadmill score for predicting prognosis in coronary artery disease.** *Ann Intern Med* 1987, **106**:793–800.

31. Marks DB *et al.*: **Prognostic value of a treadmill exercise score in out-patients with suspected coronary artery disease.** *N Engl J Med* 1991, **325**:849–853.

32. Chang J *et al.*: **Prognostic impact of myocardial ischaemia [Editorial].** *J Am Coll Cardiol* 1994, **23**: 225–228.

33. Mulcahy D *et al.*: **Asymptomatic ischaemia during daily life in stable coronary disease: relevant or redundant.** *Br Heart J* 1994, **72**:5–8.

34. Pepine CJ: **Ambulatory ischaemia.** *Eur Heart J* 1995, **16**:297–298.

35. Ghandi MM: **Ambulatory myocardial ischaemia in stable anigna.** *Br J Hosp Med* 1995, **53**:526–529.

36. Deedwania P: **Is there evidence in support of the ischaemia suppression hypothesis?** *J Am Coll Cardiol* 1994, **24**:21–24.

37. Pohost GM, Henzlova MJ: **The value of thallium-201 imaging.** *N Engl J Med* 1990, **323**:190–192.

38. Anonymous: **Thallium scintigraphy for diagnosis and risk assessment of coronary artery disease [Editorial].** *Lancet* 1991, **338**:786–788.

39. Machecourt J *et al.*: **Prognostic value of thallium-**

201 single photon emission computed tomographic myocardial perfusion imaging according to extent of myocardial defect. *J Am Coll Cardiol* 1994, **23**: 1096–1106.

40. Gill JB *et al.*: **Prognostic importance of thallium uptake by lung during exercise in coronary artery disease.** *N Engl J Med* 1987, **317**:1485–1489.

41. Weiss AT *et al.*: **Transient ischaemic dilation of the left ventricle on stress thallium-201 scintigraphy.** *J Am Coll Cardiol* 1987, **9**:752–759.

42. Pollock SG *et al.*: **Independent and incremental prognostic value of tests performed in hierarchical order to evaluate patients with suspected coronary artery disease.** *Circulation* 1992, **85**:237–248.

43. Bonow RO *et al.*: **Exercise induced ischaemia in mildly symptomatic patients with coronary artery disease and preserved left ventricular function.** *N Engl J Med* 1984, **311**:1339–1345.

44. Mukherjee S, Davidoff R: **Stress echocardiography.** *Cardiology in Review* 1993, **1**:350–362.

45. Picano E *et al.*: **Prognostic value of dipyridamole echocardiography early after uncomplicated myocardial infarction: a large scale multicenter trial.** *Am J Med* 1993, **95**:608–618.

46. Ismail G *et al.*: **Long term prognosis of patients with a normal exercise echocardiogram and clinical suspicion of myocardial ischaemia.** *Am J Cardiol* 1995, **75**:934–936.

47. Friesinger GC *et al.*: **Prognostic significance of coronary arteriography.** *Trans Assoc Am Physicians* 1970, **83**:78–82.

48. Mock MB *et al.*: **Survival of medically treated patients in the Coronary Artery Surgery Study (CASS) registry.** *Circulation* 1982, **66**:562–568.

49. Edmond M *et al.*: **Long term survival of medically treated patients in the Coronary Artery Surgery Study (CASS) registry.** *Circulation* 1994, **90**:2645–2657.

50. Chaitman BR *et al.*: **A lifetable and cox regression analysis of patients with combined proximal left anterior descending with proximal left circumflex coronary artery disease: non-left main equivalent lesions (CASS).** *Circulation* 1983, **68**:1163–1170.

51. Varnauskas E for the European Coronary Surgery Study Group. **Twelve year follow-up of survival in the randomised European Coronary Surgery Group.** *N Engl J Med* 1988, **319**:332–337.

52. Taylor HA *et al.*: **Asymptomatic left main coronary artery disease in the Coronary Artery Surgery Study (CASS) registry.** *Circulation* 1989, **79**:1171–1179.

53. Hueb W *et al.*: **Two- to eight-year survival rates in patients who refused coronary artery bypass grafting.** *Am J Cardiol* 1989, **63**:155–159.

54. Zack PM *et al.*: **Survival patterns in clinical and angiographic subsets of medically treated patients with combined proximal left descending and proximal left circumflex coronary artery disease (CASS).** *Am Heart J* 1989, **118**:220–227.

55. Little WC *et al.*: **Can coronary angiography predict the site of a subsequent myocardial infarction in patients with mild to moderate coronary artery disease?** *Circulation* 1988, **78**:1157–1166.

56. Kaiser GC *et al.*: **Survival following coronary bypass grafting in patients with severe angina pectoris (CASS).** *J Thorac Cardiovasc Surg* 1985, **89**:513–524.

57. De Trano R *et al.*: **Exercise induced ST segment depression in the diagnosis of multivessel coronary disease: a meta-analysis.** *J Am Coll Cardiol* 1989, **14**:1501–1508.

58. Braverman AC: **Risk stratification in unstable angina: role of exercise electrocardiography, thallium scintography, dipyridamole imaging and evaluation of left ventricular function.** In *Unstable Angina*. Edited by Rutherford JD. New York: Marcel Dekker; 1992: 121–141.

59. Braunwald E *et al.*: **Unstable angina: diagnosis and managment.** *Clinical Practice Guideline No. 10.* Rockville MD: Public Health Service; 1994.

60. Calvin JE *et al.*: **Risk stratification in unstable angina: prospective validation of the Braunwald classification.** *JAMA* 1995, **273**:136–141.

61. Liuzzo G *et al.*: **The prognostic value of C-reactive protein and serum amyloid A protein in severe unstable angina.** *N Engl J Med* 1994, **331**: 417–424.

62. Gottlieb SO *et al.*: **Silent ischaemia predicts infarction and death during 2 year follow up of unstable angina.** *J Am Coll Cardiol* 1987, **10**:756–760.

63. Bugiardini R *et al.*: **Angiographic morphology in unstable angina and its relation to transient myocardial ischaemia and hospital outcome.** *Am J Cardiol* 1991, **67**:460–464.

64. Scott SM *et al.*: **VA study of unstable angina: 10 year results show duration of surgical advantage for patients with impaired ejection fraction.** *Circulation* 1994, **90**:II-120–II-123.

65. Larsson H *et al.*: **Should the exercise test be performed at discharge or one month later after an episode of unstable angina or non-Q wave myocardial infarction?** *Int J Card Imaging* 1991, **7**: 7–14.

66. Thaulow E, Erikssen E: **Prognostic implications of asymptomatic cardiac ischaemia.** *Cardiology* 1994, **85(suppl 2)**:11–15.

67. Ekelund LG *et al.*: **Coronary heart disease morbidity and mortality in hypercholesterolaemic men predicted from an exercise test. The Lipid Research Clinics Coronary Primary Prevention trial.** *J Am Coll Cardiol* 1989, **14**:556–563.

68. Fleg JL *et al.*: **Prevalence and prognostic significance of exercise induced silent myocardial ischaemia detected by thallium scintigraphy and electrocardiography in asymptomatic volunteers.** *Circulation* 1990, **81**:428–436.

69. Hedblad B *et al.*: **Increased mortality in men with ST segment depression during 24 hour ambulatory long term ECG recording. Results from the prospective population study 'Men Born in 1914' from Malmo, Sweden.** *Eur Heart J* 1989, 10:149–158.

Clinical trials in stable and unstable angina
John Cleland

Introduction

Trials examining the efficacy of antianginal treatments and their effect on progression of coronary disease in stable angina are analysed in this chapter. Trials involving coronary atherosclerosis and cardiovascular prophylaxis are included because these involve patients at high risk of future development of angina.

Trials in unstable angina are discussed separately, because the pathophysiology and management of this disorder differ greatly from those of stable angina. The value of detecting 'silent' ischaemia remains in doubt [1,2]. However, its most common symptomatic presentation is angina pectoris [3,4], so a strong rationale exists for treating 'silent' and symptomatic ischaemia in a similar fashion. Angina pectoris is also the most common coronary presentation of patients at high risk of coronary disease [5].

The precise relationship between syndrome X (angina-like chest pain associated with ST-segment depression in the absence of coronary artery disease) and myocardial ischaemia remains to be clarified [6] but patients with syndrome X have a good prognosis, although they can still develop coronary disease, especially if they have the appropriate risk factors [6,7]. Syndrome X is mainly a condition of postmenopausal women. Oestrogen deficiency may be an important factor and hormone replacement therapy may be the most effective treatment for women with this disorder [6,8]. Hormone replacement therapy may also reduce the risk of coronary events in postmenopausal women without syndrome X [9,10,11].

Drug action and angina pectoris

Increased heart rate both increases myocardial oxygen requirements and reduces the duration of diastole (when most of the blood flow through the myocardium occurs) (Fig. 5.1). Thus agents that slow heart rate not only reduce myocardial oxygen demand but also increase myocardial blood flow to ischaemic areas, although resting global myocardial blood flow may fall because of autoregulation in response to the decrease in myocardial oxygen demand. However, coronary collateral flow during exercise may be adversely affected by beta blockers [12].

Most agents that reduce afterload also cause coronary vasodilatation and it is difficult to be sure which of these actions is most important. However, an excessive fall in arterial pressure may exacerbate angina, especially in the presence of a fixed coronary obstruction, which suggests that reducing arterial pressure in the absence of coronary vasodilatation may be deleterious [13].

Fig. 5.1. *Myocardial ischaemia can be caused by an excessive myocardial oxygen demand or a failure to deliver sufficient oxygen. *Potentially of special importance in patients with unstable angina; †e.g. anaemia, hypoxic lung disease.*

Increased oxygen demand	Reduced oxygen supply
Increased heart rate	Coronary atheromatous
Increased afterload	obstruction
Increased preload	Increased heart rate
Increased contractility	Increased coronary tone*
Left ventricular	Increased blood viscosity
hypertrophy	Left ventricular hypertrophy
	Reduced blood oxygen
	content†
	Maldistribution of
	intramyocardial blood flow
	Intracoronary thrombosis &
	platelet activation*
	Increased preload
	Increased coronary perfusion
	pressure (in reduced blood
	pressure)

Reducing preload reduces myocardial oxygen requirements but also could increase oxygen supply by increasing the myocardial arteriovenous pressure gradient. The reduction in preload on nitrate therapy has been held responsible for the effect of this class of drug, but diuretics also reduce preload and are not known for their antianginal effects.

Agents that reduce contractility, such as beta blockers and verapamil, are effective antianginal agents but antiarrhythmic drugs, such as flecainide and disopyramide, depress cardiac contractility and are not known for their antianginal effects. Many effective antianginal agents do not reduce contractility.

Increased coronary tone accounts for some of the day-to-day variation in the severity of stable exertional angina. Rarely, increased coronary tone or 'spasm' associated with only minor or, very rarely, no coronary disease may cause angina [14]. Prinzmetal's angina is unpredictable in its occurrence, although it may be provoked by exercise and it often wakes the patient from sleep. Increased coronary tone, due to local activation of thrombogenic factors, also plays an important role in unstable angina.

Platelet activation and coronary thrombosis may be important in the progression of stable angina pectoris and is important in unstable angina. The results of recent studies suggest that heparin analogues can reduce the frequency of stable exertional angina and can reduce symptoms in the short term in unstable angina pectoris. Aspirin is often used to treat unstable angina but has not been shown to reduce the rate of progression of atheroma [15].

Smoking may cause sympathetic nervous system activation, resulting in coronary vasoconstriction at sites of atheroma and preventing the benefits of antianginal agents

[16,17]. Smoking also releases carbon monoxide, which combines with haemoglobin to prevent oxygen uptake [18]. Nicotine patches appear safe in patients with angina and are modestly effective at helping them to stop smoking [19].

To evaluate the effects of a drug on coronary blood flow it is important to know whether the increased flow has been directed to areas of ischaemia. Dipyridamole is an effective coronary vasodilator but, in some cases, it can exacerbate angina by dilating normal arterial segments and diverting blood away from arteries with an epicardial coronary stenosis [20]. However, dipyridamole can improve angina in some patients [21]. The subendocardium has a more precarious blood supply than the epicardium and drugs may alter the balance between endocardial and epicardial blood flow. Aminophylline is a coronary vasoconstrictor that may improve angina either by constricting normal arteries to a greater extent than diseased ones, thus diverting blood supply to ischaemic areas, or by exerting a vasodilator effect on the coronary collateral supply [22,23].

Left ventricular hypertrophy increases myocardial work and oxygen demand. If the increase in microvasculature is insufficient to keep pace with the myocardial hypertrophy, the diffusion distance between capillaries and the myocyte is increased, impairing oxygen delivery [24].

Currently, medical treatment of the symptom angina is based on three classes of drugs: nitrovasodilators, beta blockers and calcium antagonists. Other classes of drugs that purport to alter myocardial metabolism or reduce the rate of discharge of the sino-atrial node are not in widespread international use and must be considered experimental at this stage. Drugs such as aminophylline [22], amiodarone [25] and heparin analogues [26,27] given subcutaneously have a limited role for use in special circumstances.

Efficacy of antianginal agents

Large studies of antianginal agents

A summary of large double-blind, multicentre studies is shown in Figure 5.2.

Smaller studies of antianginal agents

Several hundred smaller placebo-controlled clinical trials of antianginal agents in clinical use have been published [16,26,27,30,36–112].

The antianginal agent of first choice is generally a matter of personal preference, on the part of the doctor and the patient, and cost. Exceptions to this rule are the use of beta blockers in patients with asthma. Relative contraindications and side effects of antianginal agents are shown in Figure 5.3.

Study	No. of patients Follow-up Mean age	Comparison	Mean angina attacks/week (and % improved)	CABG or PTCA	MI	Deaths
CAPE 1994 [28] Double-blind	315 8 weeks 59 years	Placebo Amlodipine 10 mg od	4.0 (44%) 2.8 (70%) P<0.001	0 0	0 0	1 1
ACIP* 1994 [29] Partially-blind	618 12 weeks ND	Angina therapy Ischaemia therapy Revascular- ization	Not applicable	14 (6.9%) 8 (4.0%) 7 (3.3%)†	2 (1.0%) 2 (1.0%) 4 (1.9%)	1 0 0
TIBBS 1995 [30] Double-blind	330 8 weeks 57 years	Nifedipine SR 40 mg od Bisoprolol 10–20 mg od	Baseline 6 Low dose 4 (42%)‡ High dose 3 (49%)‡ Baseline 5 Low dose 3 (74%)‡ High dose 2 (81%)‡ P<0.001	ND	ND	ND
ASIST* 1994 [31] Double-blind	306 1 year 64 years	Atenolol 100 mg od Placebo	*Worsening angina* 9 26 P<0.01	1 0	2 3	*Death/resus* 1 4
TIBET [32,33]	682 6 weeks 60 years	Nifedipine SR Atenolol Combination	*Treatment failure or unstable angina* 8.2% 9.7% 7.1% NS	6 8 4 NS	15 14 7 NS	*Cardiac only* 6 3 4 NS
IMAGE 1995 [34]	280 6 weeks 59 years	Metoprolol CR 200 mg/day Nifedipine SR 20 mg bd	*Episodes/week* −1.7 −1.5 NS	0 1 NS	1 1 NS	ND
APSIS 1993 [35]	809 3+ years ND	Metoprolol 200 mg bd Verapamil SR 240 mg bd	Full report awaited			5.5% 6.0% NS

Fig. 5.2. *Recent large comparative trials of symptomatic efficacy of antianginal agents. *The ACIP and ASIST studies investigated patient populations with little or no symptomatic ischaemia and hence should be interpreted with caution; †second revascularization procedure; ‡percentage with >50% reduction in episodes; bd, twice daily; CR, controlled release; ND, no data; NS, not significant; od, once daily; resus, resuscitation; SR, sustained release.*

Agent	Side effect
Nitrates	Headache (start with a low doses, spit out or swallow if sublingual or buccal preparation). Tolerance (use drug-free interval). Buccal preparations are difficult to use for people with dentures. Hypotension may be a problem especially for patients with a low preload (e.g. those on diuretics).
Beta blockers	Asthma an absolute contraindication. Exacerbation of heart failure can occur, although this is not as frequent as once supposed. Exacerbation of intermittent claudication does not generally occur as once supposed. Hypotension, lethargy, muscle aches, insomnia, dreams and impotence may be considered minor side effects but can be a major problem to patients. All side effects can be managed by reducing the dose, changing the type of beta blocker or withdrawing it.
Dihydropyridine calcium antagonists, e.g. nifedipine, amlodipine	Flushing, headache and hypotension (start with small doses). Peripheral oedema (raise legs while at rest, or reduce or stop drug). Adding a beta blocker appears to reduce side effects.
Diltiazem	Generally low side effect profile. Caution advised when used with a beta blocker because combination may cause excessive bradycardia.
Verapamil	Constipation (may resolve with continued use, increase fruit in diet, long-acting preparations may be less troublesome). Avoid combination with beta blocker, unless under care of cardiologist, because of risk of bradycardia and inducing heart failure.

Fig. 5.3. *Side effects of commonly used antianginal drugs.*

Problems with commonly used antianginal agents

Smoking may negate much of the antianginal effect of calcium antagonists [16,17] but calcium antagonists may perform better than beta blockers when patients are exerting themselves during cold weather [113].

Overall, studies of antianginal agents show that increasing the dose of a single agent or combining two agents can improve effect. Chrysant *et al.* [44] suggest that nitrates, in common with many other drugs of modern practice, may be prescribed in insufficient doses.

The benefit of a third agent remains to be proved [114] but a 'try it and see' approach can be adopted, although the need for three antianginal treatments indicates that surgery for relief of symptoms should be contemplated.

Nitrates

No long-term trials of nitrates in patients with angina pectoris have been undertaken to show if they alter clinical outcome other than symptoms. Four large trials incorporating over 80 000 patients have failed to show improvement in rates of reinfarction or mortality after MI [115].

Beta blockers

No long-term trials compare beta blockers and placebo in patients with angina pectoris. The ASIST and TIBET studies [31–33] suggest that beta blockers and calcium antagonists are equally effective in reducing serious events, although the combination may be superior to either agent alone. Long-term trials after MI suggest that beta blockers reduce the risk of reinfarction and death [115]. In hypertension, the situation is less clear cut.

Effects of antianginal treatment on progression of coronary disease and mortality

Calcium antagonists

A summary of studies is shown in Figure 5.4. Calcium antagonists should not be used as monotherapy in patients with unstable angina, and should be used with caution in patients with heart failure. Dihydropyridine calcium antagonists appear safe in combination with a beta blocker in unstable angina. Evidence indicates that some dihydropyridine antagonists may be safe in patients with heart failure caused by ischaemic heart disease and may even reduce mortality in those with heart failure from other, as

Study	No. of patients Follow-up Mean age	Comparison	Nonfatal MI	Nonfatal stroke	Mortality
INTACT 1990 [116] Double-blind	425 36 months 53 years	Nifedipine 20 mg qid Placebo	ND	ND	8 2
Waters 1990 [117] Double-blind	383 24 months 51 years	Nicardipine 30 mg qid Placebo	14 8	ND	2 3
O'Keefe 1991 [118] Double-blind	201 12 months (after angioplasty) ND	Diltiazem 140–360 mg od Placebo	0 4	ND	4 1

Fig. 5.4. *Studies of the effects of calcium antagonists on the progression of coronary disease. ND, no data; od, once daily; qid, four times a day.*

67

yet unspecified, causes. No conclusive evidence exists to suggest that calcium antagonists alter prognosis in patients with angina [115,119–122].

In the long-term trials assessing the effects of calcium antagonists on the progression of coronary artery disease or restenosis after angioplasty [116,117], the event rates have been low. Any effect on angiographic progression appears small and this has not translated into a reduction in the more critical endpoints of MI or death. A useful effect on the rate of restenosis cannot be discounted but further, more substantial, clinical trials are required. Nifedipine and diltiazem do not improve prognosis after MI, but verapamil has been shown to have similar benefits to a beta blocker when introduced late after MI in patients without evidence of heart failure [115].

ACE inhibitors

A summary of studies is shown in Figure 5.5. Studies of patients with left ventricular systolic dysfunction with or without heart failure suggest that ACE inhibitors reduce recurrent MI, although the effect was not apparent until at least 1 year after treatment was started [125]. This could reflect a direct effect on coronary atherosclerosis. Postangioplasty trials do not confirm any benefit of ACE inhibitors on restenosis or serious clinical events in patients with well preserved ventricular function but their short follow-up (6 months) may account for the difference from the SOLVD study result [126]. The results of long-term studies in patients with coronary artery disease but without ventricular dysfunction, such as the QUIET study, are awaited [127,128].

Study	No. of patients Follow-up Mean age	Comparison	Nonfatal MI	Mortality
MERCATOR 1992 [123] Double-blind	735 6 months (after angioplasty) 57 years	Cilazapril 5 mg bd Placebo	5 8	3 2
MARCATOR 1995 [124] Double-blind	1426 6 months (after angioplasty) 58 years	Cilazapril 1 mg bd 5 mg bd 10 mg bd Placebo	9 8 10 8	3 2 2 1

Fig. 5.5. *Studies of the effects of ACE inhibitors on the progression of coronary disease (no data on nonfatal stroke). bd, twice a day; ND, no data.*

Fish oils, vitamins and antioxidants

A summary of studies is shown in Figure 5.6. Despite epidemiological evidence indicating that a high level of antioxidant vitamins or fish oil intake may reduce the risk of coronary disease, the randomized trials are inconclusive. A recent large

Study	No. of patients Follow-up Mean age	Study population	Comparison	MI (worsened angina)	Stroke	Mortality
PQRST 1994 [129]	303 36 months 55 years	Femoral atherosclerosis (24% had angina)	Probucol Placebo	9 (13) 8 (10)	2 0	0 2
Gapinski 1993 [130] Meta-analysis	886 ND ND	Coronary angioplasty	Fish oils 3–6.5 g/dl Control	No significant effect on frequency of positive exercise test	ND	ND
Cancer Prevention Study Group 1994 [131]	29 133 5–8 years 57 years	Male smokers Factorial design	Vitamin E No vitamin E Beta-carotene No beta-carotene	4.1% 4.4% NS 4.5% 4.0% NS	0.8% 0.8% NS 0.9% 0.7% NS	12.3% 12.1% NS 12.7%* 11.8% P=0.02
Linxian 1993 [132]	29 584 5 years 40–69 years	Factorial design	Retinol + zinc Riboflavin + niacin Vitamin C + molybdenum Beta-carotene+ vitamin E + selenium	ND	Fatal (RRR) 0.99, NS 0.93, NS 1.04, NS 0.90, NS	RRR 1.00, NS 0.97, NS 1.01, NS 0.91, P =0.03
CHAOS 1995 [133]	1429 ND 61 years	84% male Known IHD	Vitamin E 400–800 IU/dl	Interim report suggests improved infarct-free survival		
Gaziano 1990 [134]	333 ND 40–84 years	US physicians with angina or revascularization	Beta-carotene Placebo	44% reduction in all major coronary events and 49% reduction in all major vascular events		

Fig. 5.6. *Effects of fish oils, vitamins and antioxidants.*relative excess risk; IHD, ischaemic heart disease; ND, no data; NS, not significant; RRR, relative risk reduction.*

epidemiological study from the USA has failed to confirm a link between fish intake and coronary disease [134].

The effect of fish oil supplements on restenosis after angioplasty is modest and high doses, which cause side effects such as diarrhoea, belching and dysgeusia, may be required to obtain a modest 25% reduction in restenosis [130]. The evidence that reduction in angiographic stenosis is accompanied by a reduction in coronary events is questionable.

Four large studies have reported in whole [131,132] or in part [133,134] on the effects of vitamin or mineral supplements. The two largest trials were on cancer prevention but also recorded cardiovascular events.

The Cancer Prevention Group [131] investigated a well nourished Finnish population at high risk of ischaemic heart disease and found a small excess mortality with beta-carotene supplements. Vitamin E supplements led to a nonsignificant fall in fatal cardiac events and beta-carotene, a nonsignificant excess of fatal cardiac events. The Lanxian study from China [132] investigated a population with a low risk of ischaemic heart disease but with a more marginal diet and found a reduction in total mortality with a treatment combination of beta-carotene, vitamin E and selenium. The CHAOS study [133] suggests a benefit with vitamin E treatment. The US Physicians study [135] is the only one to suggest a reduction in cardiac events with beta-carotene.

Aspirin and warfarin in primary prevention

A summary of studies is shown in Figure 5.7. The two large primary prevention trials conducted with aspirin did not show a significant reduction in mortality. The US Physicians study [135] showed that the rate of MI may have been reduced but this was not accompanied by a lower mortality, suggesting that the result should be treated with caution because aspirin may have merely increased the proportion of 'silent infarcts'. No evidence indicates that aspirin saves lives when given for primary prevention and no consistent evidence that it reduces infarction. There does appear to be a small but consistent increase in haemorrhagic stroke and death. Primary prevention studies with warfarin are underway.

Study	No. of patients	Comparison	Nonfatal MI	Nonfatal stroke	Mortality
US Physicians 1989 [135,136]	22 071	Aspirin 325 mg alt die Placebo	1.2% 1.9% RRR 58% $P<0.001$	1.0% 0.8% RExR 25% NS	2.0% 2.1% RRR 5% NS
UK Physicians 1988 [141]	5139	Aspirin 500 mg/dl Placebo	2.5% 2.2% RExR 14% NS	1.7% 1.3% RExR 31% NS	7.9% 8.8% RExR 10% NS

Fig. 5.7. *Aspirin and warfarin in primary prevention. alt die, every other day; NS, not significant; RExR, relative excess risk; RRR, relative risk reduction.*

Aspirin and warfarin in chronic stable angina

A summary of studies is shown in Figure 5.8. One small trial suggested a clear mortality benefit from intense anticoagulative treatment [137]. Evidence for a mortality benefit and an effect on MI is supported by long-term trials after MI [115].

The SAPAT trial [139] indicated that aspirin reduces the risk of nonfatal MI. Trends towards a reduction in mortality or stroke were not significant. Although aspirin has clear-cut benefits early after acute MI, the results of long-term administration after MI suggest little if any mortality benefit [115]. Further trials are required before a clear mandate can be given for long-term aspirin therapy in stable angina, although, on balance, the evidence does suggest that treating 1000 patients for 1 year may save three lives and prevent five symptomatic MIs. However, the risks of gastrointestinal haemorrhage may outweigh the benefits on reduced coronary events in patients with stable coronary disease. Aspirin may have adverse effects on cardiovascular outcome in some subgroups, for instance those with coronary disease and heart failure.

Study	No. of patients Follow-up Mean age	Comparisons	Nonfatal MI	Nonfatal stroke	Mortality
Borchgrevink 1962 [137] Open label	147 32 months < 70 years	Intensive anti- coagulation Moderate anti- coagulation	2 (2.7%) 14 (19.2%) RRR 86% P < 0.001	ND	1 (1.4%) 13 (17.8%) RRR 92% P < 0.001
MAYO-B 1989 [138]	370 54 months ND	Aspirin 975 mg + dipyridamole Placebo	10 22 RRR 55% P < 0.01	0 4 NS	11 12 NS
SAPAT 1992 [139] Double-blind	2035 50 months 67 years	Aspirin 75 mg Placebo	47 (4.7%) 78 (7.6%) RRR 39% P = 0.006	28 (2.8%) 38 (3.7%) RRR 25% NS	82 (8.1%) 106 (10.3%) RRR 22% NS
Am Phys Sub Study 1993 [140] Double-blind	333 60 months 63 years	Aspirin 325 mg alt die Placebo	7 16 RRR 63% P < 0.02	4 0 NS	7 11 NS

Fig. 5.8. *Aspirin and warfarin in chronic stable angina. alt die, alternate days; MI, myocardial infarction; ND, no data; NS, not significant; RRR, relative risk reduction.*

Aspirin and warfarin after coronary artery bypass grafting (CABG)

A summary of studies is shown in Figure 5.9. Aspirin improves early graft patency after coronary artery venous grafting (CAVG) but little evidence shows that it reduces the rate of infarction and no evidence that it reduces mortality. Withdrawal studies suggest that it is not necessary to continue aspirin beyond the first year [149] or even beyond the first 3 months [148]. Graft occlusion or clinical events were no more frequent when aspirin was withdrawn in the latter studies [140,142]. This further

Study	No. of patients Follow-up Mean age	Comparison	Nonfatal MI	Nonfatal stroke	Mortality
Brooks 1985, Gerschlick 1988 [142,143] Double-blind	320 78 months 54 years	Aspirin 900 mg + dipyridamole Placebo	7 (angina, 49) 2 (angina, 45) NS	0 0	9 8 NS
Cheseboro 1984 [144] Double-blind	407 12 months 56 years	Aspirin 975 mg + dipyridamole Placebo	0 0	ND	5 6 NS
VA Co-operative 1989 [145] Double-blind	772 12 months 58 years	Aspirin ± dipyrimadole or sulphinpyrazone Placebo	6.5% 7.2% NS	5 3 NS	4.2% 3.3% NS
VA Co-operative 1994 [146] Withdrawal	334 24 months 60 years	Aspirin continued after 1 year Aspirin withdrawal	1.9% 1.7% NS	ND	1.9% 2.3% NS
CABADAS 1993 [147] Open label	948 12 months 58 years	Aspirin Aspirin + dipyridamole Oral anticoagulants	8.1% 9.8% 7.8% NS	0.3% 2.0% 1.3% NS	2.6% 1.7% 1.0% NS
Pfisterer 1989 [148] Partially-blind	249 12 months 56 years	Aspirin 50 mg + dipyridamole Phenprocoumon	6 (4 periop) 8 (all periop) NS	0 1 NS	3 8 $P < 0.05$

Fig. 5.9. *Aspirin and warfarin after CABG. Some of the mortality data have been obtained from aspirin trialists report, 1994. ND, no data; NS, not significant; periop, perioperative.*

supports the conjecture that aspirin may be helpful in the setting of acute vascular damage (i.e. MI, unstable angina, early after CAVG) but of no benefit, and possibly harmful, at other times.

Multiple risk factor intervention trials

A summary of the large trials (n > 90) is shown in Figure 5.10. The Oslo, MRFIT and WHO-Factories studies [150–156] selected groups of men who had multiple coronary risk factors and randomly allocated them to special care (aggressive management of risk factors in special clinics) or to usual care. No overall reduction in mortality or MI

Study	No. of patients Follow-up Mean age	Study population	Comparison	Stroke	MI	CHD death	Mortality
Oslo 1981 [150]	1232 60 months 45 years	Healthy men at high risk of IHD	Intervention Control	1 29	13 22 NS	8 15 NS	16 24 NS
MRFIT 1982,1990 [151,152]	12 866 126 months < 57 years	Asymptomatic men at high risk for IHD	SI UC	ND	ND	3.1% 3.5% NS	7.7% 8.3% NS
MRFIT 1985 [153]	1499 72 months ND	Substudy on asymptomatic men with positive ETT (Normal or abnormal resting ECG)	SI UC	Reduction in sudden cardiac death		17 (2.2%) 38 (5.2%) RRR 58% P<0.01	32(4.2%) 45(6.1%) RRR 31% P<0.01
WHO Factories study 1986 [154–156]	49 781 ND ND	Male	SI UC	ND	1.9% 2.1% NS	1.4% 1.5% NS	4.3% 4.4% NS
Miettinen 1985 [157]	1815 60 months 48 years	Male	High risk/SI High risk/UC Low risk	0 P<0.01 8 1	15 NS* 8 2	1 4 0	10 NS 5 3
Heidelberg 1990 [158,159]	113 12 months 54 years	Coronary atherosclerosis	Diet + exercise UC	One VT ND	0 (2UA) 3 (1UA)	2 0	2 1
SCRIP 1994 [160]	300 48 months 56 years	Coronary atherosclerosis	SI UC	ND	ND	ND	3 3

Fig. 5.10. *Multiple risk factor intervention. *High risk and special care versus high risk and usual care; ETT, exercise test tolerance; IHD, ischaemic heart disease; ND, no data;. NS, not significant; RRR, relative risk reduction; SI, special intervention; UC, usual care.*

was seen, although the Oslo trial did suggest a significant reduction in the combined endpoint. The small difference between groups in the reduction in risk factors using the two proposed strategies accounted for the failure of the study to show any difference, according to the MRFIT investigators. An MRFIT substudy, in which men with an abnormal exercise test were identified, showed that special care could reduce the risk of death. However, the 6-year follow-up showed that only a small proportion of those with a positive test had died (i.e. the predictive value of a positive test was low and of no clinical use). The trials generally suggest that the reduction in coronary events is directly related to the individual's ability to change his risk factors. In summary, the evidence in favour of multiple risk factor intervention in patients at high risk of coronary disease is fairly compelling but the magnitude of benefit in clinical practice is difficult to gauge and could be small. One study [157] suggested no benefit from special care, although this could reflect the lack of efficacy of a lipid-lowering regimen based mainly on probucol [129] and clofibrate.

Hypertensive treatment

A summary of studies is shown in Figure 5.11. Hypertension is a common antecedent of angina, especially in the elderly. After MI, evidence shows that hypertension may contribute to morbidity and mortality. Trials of hypertension in the elderly show that:

- Antihypertensive therapy reduces the risk of stroke by about 40%.

- Antihypertensive therapy reduces the risk of a coronary event by 15–20% and this is reflected by a similar reduction in total mortality.

- The relative benefits of antihypertensive therapy may be similar across different risk groups but, as the absolute risk increases, so does the absolute benefit. Some evidence suggests that the relative benefits of treatment may also be greater in higher risk patients. Thus in the SHEP study [165], the relative risk reduction of a coronary event in those with a normal baseline ECG was only 17% but, in those with an abnormal ECG (indicating more left ventricular hypertrophy and a greater probability of coronary disease), the relative risk reduction for a coronary event was 31%. Similarly, the relative risk reduction of coronary events was markedly greater in the MRC trial [166] of elderly patients with hypertension than that in the trial of younger patients [161]. The relative and absolute benefits of treatment may be greater in the elderly, who are more likely to have underlying cardiovascular disease. The benefits of treatment appear greater in men, another group at higher risk of cardiovascular events.

- Both MRC trials [161,166] suggest that the benefits of treatment of hypertension with a beta blocker is largely abolished by smoking, whereas the effects of thiazides are reduced. Smokers are at higher risk of experiencing events than non-smokers.

74

Study	No. of patients Follow-up Mean age Sex	Comparisons	Fatal and nonfatal coronary events	Fatal and nonfatal stroke	Total mortality
MRC Mild Hypertension 1985 [161] Double-blind	17 354 59 months 51 years ND	Bendrofluazide Propranolol Placebo	5.6% 4.8% 5.5% NS	0.8% 1.9% 2.6% RRR 46% $P<0.01$*	6.0% 5.5% 5.9% NS
EWPHE 1985 [162] Double-blind	840 56 months 72 years 70% female	Hydrochlorothiazide + triamterene Placebo	11.5% 13.9% NS	7.7% 11.3% RRR 32% $P=0.05$	32.5% 35.1% NS
Coope+Warrender 1986 [163] Open label	884 53 months 69 years 69% female	Active (atenolol 1st step) Control	8.4% 8.2% NS	4.8% 8.4% RRR 43% $P<0.03$	14.3% 14.8% NS
Meta-analysis 1990 [164]	36 894 ND ND ND	Active Control	3.6% 4.2% RRR 14% $P<0.01$	1.6% 2.6% RRR 42% $P<0.0001$	4.8% 5.5% RRR 13% $P<0.001$
Meta-analysis 1990 [164]	21 626 ND ND ND	Thiazide Beta blocker	2.9% 2.7% NS	1.0% 1.1% NS	*Vascular deaths* 1.7% 1.5% NS
SHEP 1991 [165] Double-blind	4736 54 months 72 years 57% female	Chlorthalidone-based Placebo	8.7% 13.4% RRR 35% $P<0.01$	4.5% 6.9% RRR 35% $P<0.01$	9.0% 10.2% RRR 11.8% NS
MRC Elderly 1991 [166] Double-blind	4396 70 months 70 years 58% female	Hydrochlorothiazide + amiloride Atenolol Placebo	7.7% $P<0.001$[†] $P<0.01$[‡] 12.8%, NS[§] 12.7% RRR 39%[†]	7.3% $P<0.05$[†] NS[‡] 9.0%, NS[§] 10.8% RRR 32%[†]	12.4% $P<0.05$[†] $P=0.07$[‡] 15.2%, NS[§] 14.2% RRR 13%[†]
STOP 1992 [167] Open label	1627 25 months 76 years 63% female	Atenolol or hydrochlorothiazide Placebo	*MI only* 3.1% 3.4% NS	3.6% 6.5% RRR 45% $P<0.01$	4.4% 7.7% RRR 43% $P<0.01$

Fig. 5.11. *Treatment of hypertension. *Active treatment versus placebo; [†]thiazide versus placebo; [‡]atenolol versus thiazide; [§]atenolol versus placebo; ND, no data; NS, not significant; RRR, relative risk reduction.*

- Thiazide diuretics may be more effective than beta blockers in reducing coronary and other cardiovascular events, despite their adverse metabolic effects.

Lipid-lowering therapy with resins or niacin or both

A summary of studies is shown in Figure 5.12. The primary prevention studies with niacin and resins fail to show a convincing reduction in mortality, although they do provide evidence for a reduction in the development of angina and MI. The modest benefits obtained with these treatments is obtained at a relatively high cost of side effects with both niacin and the resins. There is no adequate study of resins for secondary prevention after MI and niacin does not appear to have striking benefits in outcome after MI [115]. Nonetheless,

Study	No. of patients Follow-up Mean age	Study population	Comparisons	Angina	CABG	MI	Mortality
Colestipol Upjohn 1978 [168]	2278 3 years 54 years	Asymptomatic hyperlipidaemia	Colestipol Placebo	ND	ND	ND	3.2% 4.3% NS
LRC-CPP 1984 [5] Double-blind	3806 89 months ND	Asymptomatic hyperlipidaemia Total cholesterol Male > 265 mg/dl	Cholestyramine Placebo	12.4% 15.1% RRR 20% $P<0.01$	4.4% 5.9% RRR 21% $P=0.06$	6.8% 8.3% RRR 19% $P<0.05$	3.6% 3.7% RRR 7% NS
NHLBI-II 1984 [169]	116 60 months ND	Coronary atherosclerosis LDL cholesterol > 253 mg/dl	Cholestyramine Placebo	ND	ND	3 5	5 7
CLAS I 1987, CLAS II 1990 [170,171]	188 48 months 54 years	Prior CABG Total cholesterol 4.8–9.1 mmol/l	Colestipol + niacin Placebo	ND	Repeat CABG 14 15	6 3	1 1
FATS 1990 [172]	146 32 months 47 years	Coronary atherosclerosis Hyperlipidaemia Male	Niacin + colestipol Lovastatin + colestipol Conventional	ND	2 3 10	0 2 0	0 1 0
STARS 1992 [173]	90 39 months 50 years	Coronary atherosclerosis Total cholesterol >6 mmol/l	Diet + cholestyramine Diet only UC	ND	0 1 4	1 1 2	0 1 3

Fig. 5.12. *Lipid-lowering therapy with resins with or without niacin. ND, no data; NS, not significant; RRR, relative risk reduction; UC, usual care.*

treatment with niacin and a resin does appear to retard progression of coronary disease, although it did not increase the probability of graft patency 2 or 4 years after CABG [170,171].

In view of the inconclusive nature of these studies in relatively low-risk populations, no firm recommendation can be made for the use of these agents.

Lipid-lowering therapy with fibrates

A summary of studies is shown in Figure 5.13. The WHO trial [176] failed to show a difference in coronary events with clofibrate and all-cause mortality appeared to be increased in the treatment group. However, the mortality in the control group was similar to that of a low-cholesterol group and this may have confounded the study results. The results of the two smaller trials [174,175] demonstrated that patients with angina, rather than those with MI, appeared to benefit most from lipid-lowering therapy. The Helsinki trial [176] showed a reduction in coronary events and MI but failed to show a reduction in mortality. The effects of treatment took about 2 years to develop and increased thereafter. The data from the fibrate studies are conflicting but, when

Study	No. of patients Follow-up Mean age	Study population	Comparisons	MI	Unstable angina or CABG	Mortality
Scottish Sóc Physicians 1971 [174]	717 ~ 6 years 52 years	Angina or MI ± hyperlipidaemia 40–69 years	Clofibrate Placebo	7.1% 11.2% NS	ND	Cardiac only* 9.7% 10.4% NS
Newcastle 1971 [175]	497 ~ 5 years 52 years	Angina or MI ± hyperlidipaemia < 65 years	Clofibrate Corn oil	12.3% 18.2% P = 0.055	ND	Cardiac only* 11.1% 19.0% RRR 47% P = 0.02
WHO 1978 [176] Double-blind	10 627 64 months 46 years	Asymptomatic hyperlipidaemia Male	Clofibrate Placebo (olive oil capsules) Low cholesterol	Coronary events 3.1% 3.9% ND	ND	2.4% P < 0.01† 1.6% 1.4%
Helsinki 1987 [177]	4081 60 months 47 years	Asymptomatic hyperlipidaemia	Gemfibrozil Placebo	2.2% 3.5% RRR 37% P < 0.02	7 6	2.2% 2.1%

Fig. 5.13. *Lipid-lowering therapy with fibrates. *No difference in noncardiac death between active and control; †versus placebo; ND, no data; NS, not significant; RRR, relative risk reduction.*

considered with data from studies after MI [115], they support the use of fibrates in patients in relatively high-risk subgroups, such as those with angina. There is conflicting evidence to suggest that there may be a higher risk of rhabdomyolysis in patients treated with a statin and a fibrate [178,179].

Lipid lowering therapy with statins

A summary of studies (with n > 500) is shown in Figure 5.14. Studies with statins in various populations with established vascular disease show marked and consistent

Study	No. of patients Follow-up Mean age	Study population	Comparisons	Need for CABG or angioplasty	MI	Mortality
ACAPS 1994 [180] Double-blind	919 34 months 62 years	Carotid atheroscerosis Fasting LDL 130–189 mg/dl	Lovastatin 20–40 mg/dl Placebo	ND	5 5	1 8 $P = 0.02$
PMNSG 1993 [181]	1062 6 months 55 years	40% angina 34% previous MI	Pravastatin Placebo	ND	0 6 $P = 0.03$	0 3
REGRESS 1995 [182]	885 24 months ND	Coronary atherosclerosis 100% angina 47% previous MI Total cholesterol 4–8 mmol/l	Pravastatin Placebo	44 69	7 12	5 7
EXCEL 1994 [183]	8245 48 weeks ND	Primary prevention Hyperlipidaemia	Lovastatin 20–40 mg bd Placebo	ND	ND	3 1
Meta-analysis of small trials 1995 [184]	ND ND ND	ND	Treatment Placebo	ND	26 32 RRR 19% NS	1.1% 2.0% RRR 44% $P < 0.01$
4S 1994 [185]	4444 64 months 58 years	~ 900 angina only ~ 3500 post MI Total cholesterol 5.5–8.0 mmol/l	Simvastatin 20 or 40 mg Placebo	11.3% 17.2% RRR 37% $P < 0.00001$	15.9% 22.6% RRR 37% $P < 0.00001$	8.2% 11.5% RRR 30% $P = 0.0003$
WOSCOPS 1995 [186]	6595 59 months 55 years	Primary prevention Hyperlipidaemia	Pravastatin 40 mg Placebo	1.7% 2.5% RRR 37% $P = 0.009$	4.6% 6.5% RRR 31% $P = 0.001$	13.2% 4.1% RRR 21% $P = 0.051$

Fig. 5.14. *Lipid-lowering therapy with statins. bd, twice daily; ND, no data; NS, not significant; RRR, relative risk reduction.*

trends towards improvement in angina, reduction in the need for interventions and reductions in MI, stroke and mortality [180–190]. The 4S study [185] confirmed the trends observed in previous smaller studies. The effects of statins on mortality and morbidity are somewhat greater than the prognostic benefits of mechanical revascularization and less expensive over 5 years [191]. The benefits in at risk populations without known vascular disease, who are therefore at lower risk, are now established. The cost-effectiveness of primary prevention remains an issue.

Overview of lipid-lowering trials (including postinfarction trials)

A summary of studies is shown in Figure 5.15. An overview of the effects of different strategies to lower cholesterol show that the benefits are less certain in primary prevention trials than in secondary prevention trials. In secondary prevention trials, statins performed better than diet or nonstatin drugs in terms of relative risk reduction. However, the trials of nonstatin drugs were conducted in an era when the mortality from MI was probably higher than it is now. As the absolute risk in these trials was greater, so the absolute benefit was just as great as with diet or statins.

Coronary bypass surgery

A summary of studies is shown in Figure 5.16. The prognostic benefits of CAVG appear greatest in patients who are most symptomatic (Fig. 5.17).

Intervention	Follow-up Mean age	Comparisons	No. of patients	CHD	Total mortality
Primary prevention Diet	6 years 47 years	Diet Control	36 569 37 088	3.3% 3.2% RExR 3%	4.2% 3.9% RExR 8%
Nonstatin drugs*	5 years 46 years	Drug Control	13 493 13 997	8.4% 11.0% RRR 24%	7.0% 7.8% RRR 10%
Secondary prevention Diet	3 years 61 years	Diet Control	3291 2303	9.7% 15.3% RRR 37%	15.4% 18.5% RRR 19%
Nonstatin drugs	5 years 54 years	Drug Control	4205 4771	24.6% 29.3% RRR 16%	16.6% 18.6% RRR 11%
Statins	4 years 58 years	Drug Control	3963 3945	24% 33% RRR 27%	5.1% 7.4% RRR 31%

Fig. 5.15. *Overview of lipid lowering trials. *See Fig. 5.14 for WOSCOPS data; RExR, relative excess risk; RRR, relative risk reduction. Adapted with permission from Holme [192] and Cleland [115].*

Study recruitment details	No. of patients Follow-up Mean age	Comparisons	Persisting angina	Nonfatal MI	Mortality
Veterans 1972–74 [193–196]	686 7, 11 + 18 years 51 years	CAVG	*Severity score* 4.2 at 1 year 6.0 at 5 years 6.4 at 10 years	19% at 1 year 24% at 5 years 36% at 10 years	23% at 7 years 42% at 11 years 70% at 18 years
No angina/ CCS I 30% CCS II 40% CCS III 50%		Initial medical therapy	8.7 at 1 year $P < 0.001$ 7.8 at 5 years $P < 0.001$ 6.4 at 10 years NS	7% at 1 year $P < 0.01$ 24% at 5 years NS 31% at 10 years NS	30% at 7 years RRR 23% $P = 0.04$ 43% at 11 years RRR 2%, NS 67% at 18 years RExR 4%, NS
European 1973–1976 [197–199]	767 5 + 12 years < 65 years	CAVG	41% at 1 year 52% at 5 years	15% at 5 years (3.3% periop)	8% at 5 years 23% at 12 years
CCS I/II 57% CCS III 42% Ejection fraction >50%		Initial medical therapy	85% at 1 year 70% at 5 years	11% at 5 years NS	16% at 5 years RRR 53% $P < 0.0001$ 33% at 12 years RRR 12% $P = 0.04$
CASS 1975–1979 [200–202]	780 5, 7 + 10 years 51 years	CAVG	32% at 1 year 42% at 5 years	14% at 5 years	7.4% at 5 years 11.0% at 7 years 18.5% at 10 years
No angina 22% CCSI/II 78% CCSIII 0%		Initial medical therapy	71% at 1 year $P < 0.0001$ 64% at 5 years $P = 0.02$	11% at 5 years NS	9.2% at 5 years NS 13.6% at 7 years NS 21.3% at 10 years NS
Meta-analysis 1994 [203]	2649 5, 7 + 10 years ~ 53 years	CAVG	7.1% perioperative infarct rate	14.2% at 5 years	10.2% at 5 years 15.8% at 7 years 26.4% at 10 years
		Initial medical therapy		14.9% at 5 years NS	15.8% at 5 years RRR 39% $P < 0.0001$ 21.7% at 7 years RRR 32% $P < 0.001$ 30.5% at 10 years RRR 17% $P = 0.03$

Fig. 5.16. *Studies of coronary bypass surgery. CCS, Canadian Cardiovascular Society Angina Class; ND, no data; NS, not significant; periop, perioperative; RExR, relative excess risk; RRR, relative risk reduction.*

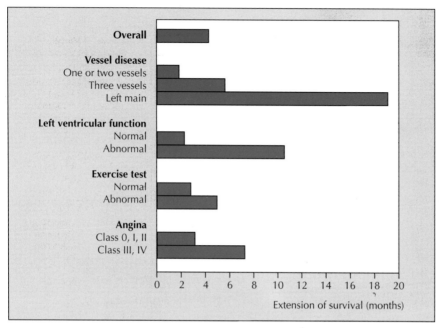

Fig. 5.17. *The prognostic benefits of CAVG appear greatest in those who are most symptomatic [203].*

Coronary surgery has improved, resulting in a decline in perioperative mortality (related to age) and improved graft patency with the use of arterial conduits. However, more aggressive medical therapy and the use of aspirin and lipid-lowering drugs may have balanced any improvements in surgical technique. The patient population has also changed. Patients over the age of 65 years, who were generally excluded from the randomized trials, have a poorer prognosis than younger patients but also a higher operative mortality and possibly greater prognostic benefit from surgery [204]. More surgical trials are required to establish the true place of surgery in clinical practice.

Many patients still require CAVG for the relief of angina. The surgical trials suggest that, compared with medical therapy, the symptomatic benefits of CAVG are markedly reduced at 5-year follow-up. Further investigation is required but aggressive medical therapy of hypertension and hyperlipidaemia will hopefully prolong the benefits of surgery.

Angioplasty

A summary of studies is shown in Figure 5.18. Patients in the ACME trial [205] assigned to PTCA had less severe angina than those assigned to medical therapy at 6 months. The PTCA group spent about twice as long in hospital and most were still taking antianginal medications at 6 months. Analysis of trends suggested that by 9–12 months there would be little difference in angina severity between the medical and PTCA

81

Study	No. of patients Follow-up Mean age	Comparisons	Persisting angina	CABG	PTCA	Nonfatal MI	Total mortality
ACME 1992 [205]	212 6 months 63 years	PTCA Medical therapy	36% 54% P < 0.01	7% 0% P < 0.01	15% 10% NS	5 3 NS	0 1 NS
RITA 1993 [206]	1011 30 months ~58 years	PTCA CABG	31% 22% P < 0.007	19% 1% P < 0.001	18% 3% P< 0.01	6.7% 5.2% NS	3.1% 3.6% NS
GABI 1994 [207]	359 12 months < 75 years	PTCA CABG	29% 26% NS	23% 1% P<0.001	28% 4% P< 0.01	7 13 NS	4 9 NS
EAST 1994 [208]	392 36 months 62 years	PTCA CABG	20% 12% P = 0.04	22% 1% P<0.001	41% 13% P<0.01	14.6% 19.6% NS	7.1% 6.2% NS
Goy 1994 [209]	134 24 months 56 years	PTCA LIMA	23% 11% P = 0.07	13% 0% P<0.01	12% 3% P<0.01	11.8% 3.0% P < 0.05	3 1 NS
CABRI 1995 [210]	1054 12 months ND	PTCA CABG	33% 25% P < 0.05	16% 1% P < 0.01	21% 3% P< 0.01	4.9% 3.5% NS	3.9% 2.7% NS
Meta analysis 1995 [211]	3371 12 months ND	PTCA CABG	CCS II or more 18% 11% P < 0.001	18% 2% P< 0.001	16% 1% P<0.001	56 54 NS	79 73 NS
BENESTENT 1994 [212]	520 7 months 58 years	Stent PTCA	26% 32% NS	6% 4% NS	14% 23% P< 0.01	4.2% 4.6% NS	2 1 NS
Stent Restenosis Study 1994 [213]	410 6 months 60 years	Stent PTCA	21% 29% NS	5% 8% NS	11% 12% NS	3.4% 3.5% NS	1.5% 1.5% NS
Adelman 1993 [214]	274 6 months 57 years	Atherectomy Angioplasty	30%* 20%* NS	23% 22% NS	6% 8% NS	4.3% 5.2% NS	1 0 NS
CAVEAT I 1993, 1995 [215,216]	1012 6 months 59 years	Atherectomy Angioplasty	30% 32% NS	8% 7% NS	28% 30% NS	7.6% (8.9%[†]) 4.4% (4.4%[†]) P = 0.04 (P=0.005[†])	1.6% (2.2%[†]) 0.6% (0.6%[†]) NS (RExR 64%[†]) (P = 0.035[†])

Study	No. of patients Follow-up Mean age	Comparisons	Persisting angina	CABG	PTCA	Non-fatal MI	Total mortality
CAVEAT II 1995 [217]	305 6 months 65 years	Atherectomy Angioplasty	42% 40%	6% 5% NS	19% 26% *P* < 0.05	20.2% 16.3% NS	7 (4.7%) 12 (7.7%) NS
Jollis (US Medicare) 1994 [218] Angioplasty Registry	217 836 ND ND	High vol centre Low vol centre Nonacute MI[‡] Acute MI[‡] 65–74 years[‡] >75 years[‡]	ND	*Emergency* 3.5% 5.3% 3.4% 3.7% 3.6% 3.0%	ND	ND	*Inhospital* 2.7% 3.7% 1.0% 6.4% 2.0% 4.8%

Fig. 5.18. *Studies of angioplasty. *Canadian Cardiovascular Society Angina Class (CCS) III/IV ; [†]at 1 year; [‡]high volume centres only; LIMA, laser beam ionization mass spectrometry analysis; ND, no data; NS, not significant; RExR, relative excess risk; RRR, relative risk reduction.*

groups [219]. No evidence exists of a prognostic advantage of PTCA over medical therapy and the US Medicare data suggest a substantial procedural morbidity and mortality from angioplasty.

In the short term, angioplasty is associated with a shorter hospital stay than CABG, with a roughly equivalent reduction in angina. In the longer term, CABG is associated with less recurrent angina, a lower need for repeat procedures and possibly a lower rate of MI. Thus PTCA is the more innocuous procedure but CABG the more definitive. PTCA is less costly in the short term but the reverse is probably true in the long term. The studies do not show any striking difference between the effect of PTCA and surgery on mortality.

Studies comparing angioplasty with stents or atherectomy devices do not show improvement in patient morbidity or mortality with the newer procedures. In fact, atherectomy may increase event rate and cost despite a slightly lower rate of restenosis. The lower rate of restenosis with stents has not translated into greater clinical benefit, although a reduction in the need for repeat angioplasty was seen in one study. A possible role for atherectomy in the management of saphenous vein graft lesions remains [217].

Prevention of restenosis after angioplasty

A summary of the studies is shown in Figure 5.19. The angioplasty trials suggest that aspirin and glycoprotein IIb/IIIa receptor blocker can reduce the risk of acute occlusion but do little to reduce the rate of subsequent restenosis [220,221]. The routine use of heparin for 24 h after angioplasty is associated with a significant increase in bleeding problems and no reduction in coronary events or restenosis. However, patients in the heparin trials who suffered a tear or dissection were generally continued on heparin

Study	No. of patients Follow-up Mean age	Comparison	Emergency (PTCA) or CABG	Restenosis	MI	Procedural mortality
Schwartz 1988 [220]	376 4–7 months 52 years	Aspirin + dypiridamole Placebo	9 9	38% 39%	1.6% 6.9 % P = 0.01	0 0
EPIC (a) 1994 [221] Double-blind High-risk angioplasty	2099 30 days 61 years	*Glycoprotein IIb/IIIa receptor blocker** Bolus Infusion Placebo	(3.6%) 2.3% (0.8%) 2.4% (4.5%, P < 0.01) 3.6%, NS	ND	6.2% 5.2% 8.6% P < 0.01	1.3% 1.7% 1.7%
EPIC (b) 1994 [221] Double-blind	1825 From 30 days until 6 months 61 years	*Glycoprotein IIb/IIIa receptor blocker* Bolus Infusion Placebo	(14.3%) 6.0% (10.1%) 4.7% (12.6%, NS) 5.6%, NS	ND	1.9% 1.7% 2.0% NS	*0–6 months* 2.6% 3.1% 3.4% NS
IMPACT 1994 [222]	150 30 days ND	*Glycoprotein IIb/IIIa receptor blocker* Bolus Infusion Placebo	(0[†]) 0 (0[†]) 1 (1[†]) 0	ND	0 0 2	0 0 0
Ellis 1989 [223]	416 6 months ND	Heparin for 24 h[‡] Placebo[‡]	(1.8%[†]) 2 (2.4%[†]) 1 NS	41.2% 36.7%	0 0 NS	ND
ERA 1994 [224]	458 6 months 58 years	Heparin[‡] Placebo[‡]	(7) 2 (5) 0	27% 29%	5 4	1 1

Study	No. of patients Follow-up Mean age	Comparison	Emergency (PTCA) or CABG	Restenosis	MI	Procedural mortality
Urban 1988 [225]	110 5 months 57 years	Warfarin Control	(15%) 4% (17% NS) 2% NS	Persisting symptoms 43% On angiography 29% Persisting symptoms 43% NS On angiography 37%, NS	ND	0 0
Gapinski 1993 [130]	886 ND ND	Fish oil	ND	Exercise test ARD 5.1% NS Angiography ARD 13.9% $P < 0.03$	ND	ND
Gershlick 1994 [226]	135 6 months 55 years	Prostacyclin (36 h) Placebo	2[§] 2 3[§] 1	Worse angina 22% Restenosis 29% Worse angina 12%, NS Restenosis 38%, NS	ND	0 3
Hillegass 1994 [227] Meta-analysis	919 patients in 5 trials ND ND	Calcium antagonists Placebo	ND	30% 38% RRR 30%, $P < 0.01$	ND	ND
Weintraub 1994 [228] Double-blind	404 6 months ND	Lovastatin 40 mg Placebo	17[§] 9 16[§] 7	44% 46% NS	14 5 $P = 0.06$	3 1
BENESTENT 1994 [212]	520 7 months 58 years	Stent PTCA	(0.4%) 1.9% (1.2%), NS 1.6%, NS	22% 32% $P = 0.02$	3.4%[§] 3.1% NS	0[§] 0
Stent Restenosis Study 1994 [213]	410 6 months 60 years	Stent PTCA	3.4%[§] 2.4% 1.5%[§] 4.0%	32% 42% $P < 0.05$	5.4%[†] 5.0% NS	0%[†] 1.5% NS
Adelman 1993 [214]	274 6 months 57 years	Atherectomy Angioplasty	4.3%[§] 1.4% 5.1%, NS[§] 4.4%, NS	46% 42% NS	4.3%[†] 3.7% NS	0[†] 0 NS
CAVEAT I 1993 [215]	1012 6 months ND	Atherectomy Angioplasty	7%[§] 3% 3%[§] 2%	50% 57% NS	6%[†] 3% NS	0%[†] 0.4% NS

Fig. 5.19. *Prospective, controlled trials of prevention of restenosis after angioplasty.*
[*]treatment in addition to aspirin and heparin; [†]procedural; [‡]treatment in addition to aspirin; [§]acute occlusions; ARD, absolute rate difference; ND, no data; NS, not significant; RRR, relative risk reduction.

85

regardless of original treatment allocation. Long-term administration of heparin does not appear to reduce the risk of restenosis.

Intracoronary stenting does appear to reduce the risk of restenosis but there is little evidence of greater clinical benefit. Calcium antagonists may be moderately effective in reducing restenosis, although a benefit on clinical outcomes has not been ascertained. Trials with fish oils suggest a modest reduction in angiographic restenosis but this has not been shown to be translated into a lower risk of angina or need for further intervention. Statins have not influenced the course of restenosis favourably.

Classification of unstable angina

Various definitions of unstable angina exist. The classification proposed by Braunwald *et al.* [229] has much to commend it, both clinically and for research purposes, but has rarely been used so far (Fig. 5.20).

Clinical trials in unstable angina

Antithrombotic agents

A summary of studies is shown in Figure 5.21. Two studies [234,238] suggest that the combination of aspirin and heparin is the most effective initial therapy for unstable angina. This is supported by the results of two smaller studies [236,237]. Use of aspirin

Severity of angina	Noncoronary aggravating factors present* (secondary unstable angina)	No aggravating factors present (primary unstable angina)	Postinfarction unstable angina (within 2 weeks)
I Accelerated angina or new-onset severe angina	IA	IB	IC
II Subacute angina at rest (within past month but no pain within past 48 h)	IIA	IIB	IIC
III Acute angina at rest (pain within past 48 h)	IIIA	IIIB	IIIC

A subscript is also designated depending on whether the patient is on 1, no antianginal treatment; 2, treatment for stable angina; 3, maximal antianginal treatment. Hence a post-MI patient having rest angina within the past 48 h on maximal therapy would be classified as $IIIC_3$. *atrial fibrillation, thyrotoxicosis, chest infection, anaemia.

Fig. 5.20. *Braunwald's classification of unstable angina. Adapted with permission from Narang [230].*

with heparin prevents the reactivation of unstable angina when heparin is discontinued. Intravenous bolus heparin may be less effective than heparin given subcutaneously or by continuous infusion.

Aspirin therapy should be continued for at least 3 months. The RISC and Veterans trials [232,238,239] show little benefit from aspirin continued thereafter.

Study	No. of patients Follow-up Mean age	Comparison	CABG or PTCA	Nonfatal MI (late)	Mortality
Telford 1981 [231] Double-blind	214 8 weeks 55 years	Heparin Atenolol Combination Placebo	2 6 2 2 NS	1 (1) 8 (2) 2 (3) 9 (1) $P = 0.024$	0 3 0 2 NS
Veterans 1983 [232] Double-blind	1266 3 months 56 years	Aspirin Placebo	2.6% 4.4% $P = 0.08$ NS	3.4% 6.9% RRR 51% $P < 0.005$	1.6% (5.5%)* 3.3% (9.6%)* RRR 51% (RRR 43%) $P = 0.054$ ($P = 0.008$*)
Canadian Multicentre 1985 [233]	555 18 months ND	Aspirin Sulphinpyrazone Combination Placebo	ND	9 7 8 7 NS	9, RRR 43% 15 7 13 $P = 0.035$
Theroux 1988, 1992 [234,235]	479 6 days ND	Aspirin Heparin (bolus + infusion) Combination Placebo	20, RRR 33% 10, RRR 69%[†] 13, RRR 60%[†] 27	4, RRR 71% 1, RRR 94%[†] 2, RRR 88%[†] 14	0 0 0 2
Serneri 1990 [236]	581 1 month ND	Aspirin 325 mg/day Intermittent heparin iv Heparin iv infusion	Only heparin by infusion appeared to be effective at reducing the frequency of angina and silent ischaemic episodes.		
SESAIR 1995 [237] Double-blind	108 1 month 64 years	Aspirin 325 mg/day Heparin sc 5000–10000 U tid for 3 days Heparin iv infusion	Heparin sc and iv infusion were equally effective at reducing ischaemic episodes. Both were better than aspirin.		

cont.

Study	No. of patients Follow-up Mean age	Comparison	CABG or PTCA	Nonfatal MI (late)	Mortality
RISC A 1990 [238] Double-blind	796 3 months ND	Aspirin 75 mg/day Heparin repeated iv bolus (5 days) Combination Placebo	ND	ND	*MI/death* 7 at 5 days 9 at 1 month RRR 68%, P < 0.004 14 at 3 months RRR 60%, P < 0.005 11 at 5 days 25 at 1 month (heparin only for 5 days) 33 at 3 months 3 at 5 days RRR 75%, P < 0.03 8 at 1 month RRR 71%, P < 0.0005 12 at 3 months RRR 66%, P < 0.0007 12 at 5 days 28 at 1 month 35 at 3 months
RISC B 1991 [239] Double-blind	796 1 year ND	Aspirin Placebo Most of benefit in first 3 months	83 116 P < 0.008	33 67 P < 0.0001	11 18 NS
European Cooperative 1994 [240]	60 Hospital stay[†] ND	Glycoprotein IIb/IIIa receptor blocker until 1 h after angioplasty Placebo	0 4 NS	1 4 NS	0 1 NS
HELVETICA 1995 [241]	1141 6 months[‡] ND	Hirudin iv infusion Hirudin iv infusion + sc Heparin	Prolonged use of hirudin associated with an incidence of death, MI or need for revascularization of 5.6% versus 11% for heparin at 4 days. No differences at 7 months. No effect on restenosis.		

Fig. 5.21. *Studies of antithrombotic agents. *Aspirin was discontinued after 12 weeks in this study but the patients were followed for 1 year; the benefits of the 12-week course of aspirin persisted despite discontinuation and it is not clear that continuation of the aspirin would have led to any greater benefit. †P < 0.01; ‡all patients had elective angioplasty 18–24 h after randomization; iv, intravenous; ND, no data; NS, not significant; RRR, relative risk reduction; sc, subcutaneous.*

This is consistent with the lack of increase in events when aspirin was withdrawn 6 weeks after MI in ISIS-2 [242]. These data support the contention that a course of aspirin, rather than life-long treatment, is all that is required after an episode of unstable angina.

Although it is currently fashionable to intervene early with surgery or angioplasty for patients with unstable angina, the good prognosis of the patients in these studies indicates that this may not be the best course of action for a patient who settles rapidly on medical therapy. As with stable angina, failure of medical therapy is the strongest argument for the need for intervention.

Calcium antagonists and beta blockers

A summary of studies is shown in Figure 5.22. Beta blockers and calcium antagonists do not produce a marked reduction in the coronary event rate, although monotherapy with short-acting nifedipine may be associated with some increase in risk. Beta blockers are indicated for use as first-line antianginal agents; if contraindications exist, verapamil [250,251] or diltiazem [244] should be given, reserving dihydropyridines for later use in combination with a beta blocker. There is evidence that addition of nifedipine to a beta blocker is safe and more effective than increasing the dose of beta blocker [247,251,252]. The different classes of calcium antagonist agents have not been compared and there are no substantial trial data on the use of intravenous nitrates for unstable angina, although they are accepted background therapy.

Coronary bypass surgery and angioplasty

These trials are summarized in Figure 5.23. They show little evidence that surgery improves prognosis in unstable angina, although patients with impaired left ventricular function may benefit [252]. In the Veterans trial [258], patients with unstable angina were deemed to be type I if pre-existing angina had worsened or new-onset angina had occurred within 2 months or type II if angina occurred frequently at rest. The short-term prognosis of type II angina is worse than that for type I, although the prognosis over 1–2 years is similar. Cross-over rates to surgery were 19.1% for type II and 5.8% for type I at 30 days. Thereafter, cross-over rates for these two groups were similar: 34% at 2 years and 45% at 8 years. In the NHLBI study [255], only 3% of those assigned to medical therapy had CABG during their initial admission but this rose to 31% by 2 years.

The surgical trials suggest that operating to relieve symptoms is an adequate strategy and that little more is to be gained prognostically by a more aggressive approach. Many patients with unstable angina settle with appropriate medical therapy [259].

Surprisingly, in the TIMI-IIIB study [257], average initial hospital stay was not reduced by an early invasive strategy for unstable angina (average 10 days), although the risk of readmission during the following 6 weeks was reduced from 14.1% to 7.8% ($P < 0.001$). At 6 weeks, the percentage of patients who were angina-free was similar (71% conservative, 76% early invasive). Of those randomly allocated to conservative management, 90% had angiography before discharge and, although the rate of PTCA was somewhat lower than in the early invasive group, the rates of CABG by 6 weeks

89

Study	No. of patients Follow-up Mean age	Comparison	Nonfatal MI (late)	CABG or PTCA	Mortality
Telford 1981 [231] Double-blind	214 (61% men) 2 months 55 years	Heparin Atenolol Combination Placebo	1 (1) 8 (2) 2 (3) 9 (1) P = 0.024	2 6 2 2 NS	0 3 0 2 NS
Gerstenblith 1982 [243]	138 4 months 61 years	Propranolol + nifedipine Propranolol + placebo	11 12 NS	26% 41% P = 0.04	7 5 NS
Andre-Fouet 1983 [244]	70 2 days ~60 years	Diltiazem Usual care	Similar benefit was achieved from diltiazem and propranolol but those patients with exclusively rest angina benefited more from diltiazem		
Muller 1984 [245]	126 14 days ~60 years	Nifedipine Propranolol + ISDN	9 9	ND	4 (8% at 6 months) 0 (3% at 6 months)
			Propanolol effective first line but adding nifedipine better than increasing propanolol		
Theroux 1985 [246]	100 5.1 months 54 years	Diltiazem Usual care	10% 8% NS	42% 38% NS	4% 4% NS
HINT (a) 1986 [247]	388 2 days ~60 years	Nifedipine Metoprolol Combination Placebo	Recurrent ischaemia or MI 47% 28% 30% 37%	Total (Q-wave) MI 28%* (16%) 16% (8%) 14% (8%) 15% (11%)	1 0 0 2
HINT (b) 1986 [247]	177 2 days ~60 years	Previous beta blocker + nifedipine Beta blocker alone	Recurrent ischaemia or MI 30% 51% P < 0.05	Total (Q-wave) MI 14% (6%) 20% (7%) NS	0 0
Hohnloser 1991 [248] Double-blind	113 72 h 62 years	Esmolol Placebo	1 3	2 6	0 0

Fig. 5.22. *Studies of calcium antagonists and beta blockers. *P < 0.01 versus placebo; NS, not significant; ISDN, isosorbide dinitrate. Data obtained from Held et al. [249].*

Study	No. of patients Follow-up Mean age	Comparison	Final angina status	Nonfatal MI (inhospital or late)	Mortality (inhospital or late)
Selden 1975 [253]	40 4 months 52 years	Surgery Medical therapy	CCS Class I/II 19 III/V 1 I/II 7 III/IV 12 P < 0.01	3 2	1 0
Pugh 1978 [254]	27 18 months 50 years	Surgery Medical therapy	CCS Class I/II 5 III/IV 0 I/II 8 III/IV 5	2 1	1 2
NHLBI 1978 [255]	288 2 years 53 years	Surgery Medical	CCS Class III/IV year 1 ~14% III/IV year 2 ~14% III/IV year 1 ~40% III/IV year 2 ~18%	30% (17/13) 19% (8/11) P < 0.05	10%(5/5) 10% (3/7) NS
Veterans 1987 [256]	468 8 years 56 years	Surgery Medical therapy	80% improved at 3 months 58% improved at 3 months	30 days 11.7% 3 years 14.7% 8 years 17.3% 30 days 4.6% P < 0.01 3 years 14.8% NS 8 years 19.0% NS	30 days 4.1% 3 years 8.7% 8 years 28% 30 days 2.1% NS 3 years 12.2% NS? 8 years 29% NS
TIMI IIIB 1994 [257]	1473 6 weeks 59 years	Early invasive Conservative	PTCA 38% CABG 25% PTCA 26% P < 0.001 CABG 24%, NS	5.7% 5.1%, NS	2.4% 2.5%, NS

Fig. 5.23. *Studies of coronary bypass surgery and angioplasty. NS, not significant.*

were similar. Even the conservative arm of this trial would be considered too aggressive by many.

Thrombolytic agents

A summary of studies is shown in Figure 5.24. Several trials suggest that thrombolytic therapy is of no value, and even harmful, in patients with unstable angina. The TIMI-IIIB trial [260] included patients with unstable angina or non-Q-wave infarction and showed an increased risk of nonfatal MI. This effect was especially marked in those with unstable angina. A trend towards a reduction in mortality was seen in patients with non-Q-wave infarction and an increase in those with unstable angina ($P = 0.07$).

Study	No. of patients Follow-up Mean age	Comparison	CABG or PTCA	Nonfatal MI	Mortality
Waters + Lam 1992 [260] Meta-analysis	523 ND ND	Thrombolysis Control	ND	22% 10% $P < 0.05$	ND
TAUSA 1994 [261]	469 Inhospital ND	Urokinase Placebo	5.2% 2.1% NS	2.6% 2.1% NS	0 0 NS
TIMI IIIB 1994 [257]	1473 6 weeks 59 years	t-PA Placebo	ND	7.4% 4.9% $P < 0.04$	2.3% 2.0% NS

Fig. 5.24. *Studies of thrombolytic agents. ND, no data; NS, not significant; t-PA, tissue plasminogen activator.*

References

1. Kohli RS et al.: **The ST segment of the ambulatory electrocardiogram in a normal population.** *Br Heart J* 1988, **60**:4–16.

2. Mulcahy D et al.: **Detection of ambulatory ischaemia is not of practical clinical value in the routine management of patients with stable angina.** *Eur Heart J* 1995, **16**:317–324.

3. Fleg JL et al.: **Prevalence and prognostic significance of exercise-induced silent myocardial ischaemia detected by thallium scintigraphy and electrocardiography in asymptomatic volunteers.** *Circulation* 1990, **81**:428–436.

4. McHenry PL et al.: **The abnormal exercise electrocardiogram in apparently healthy men: a predictor of angina pectoris as an initial coronary event during long-term follow-up.** *Circulation* 1984, **70**:547–551.

5. Lipid Research Clinics Program: **The Lipid Research Clinics Coronary Primary Prevention Trial results. I. Reduction in incidence of coronary heart disease.** *JAMA* 1984, **251**:351–363.

6. Kaski JC et al.: **Cardiac syndrome X: clinical characteristics and left ventricular function.** *J Am Coll Cardiol* 1995, **25**:807–814.

7. Lichtlen PR et al.: **Long-term prognosis of patients with angina-like chest pain and normal coronary angiographic findings.** *J Am Coll Cardiol* 1995, **25**:1013–1018.

8. Rosano GMC et al.: **Syndrome-X in women is associated with oestrogen deficiency.** *Eur Heart J* 1995, **16**:610–614.

9. Manolio TA et al.: **Associations of postmenopausal estrogen use with cardiovascular disease and its risk factors in older women.** *Circulation* 1993, **88**: 2163–2171

10. Bernardo R et al.: **Postmenopausal estrogen use and heart disease risk factors in the 1980s.** *JAMA* 1989, **261**:2095–2100

11. Stamper MJ et al.: **Postmenopausal estrogen therapy and cardiovascular disease. Ten-year follow-up from the nurses' health study.** *N Engl J Med* 1991, **325**:756–762.

12. Traverse JH et al.: **Effect of beta-adrenergic receptor blockade on blood flow to collateral-dependent myocardium during exercise.** *Circulation* 1995, **91**:1560–1567.

13. Schulz W et al.: **Relation of antianginal efficacy of nifedipine to degree of coronary arterial narrowing and to presence of coronary collateral vessels.** *Am J Cardiol* 1985, **55**:26–32.

14. Maseri A et al.: **Variant angina: one aspect of a continuous spectrum of vasospastic myocardial ischemia. Pathogenetic mechanisms, estimated incidence, clinical and coronary angiographic findings in 138 patients.** *Am J Cardiol* 1978, **42**:1019.

15. Cleland JGF, Krikler DM: **Modification of atherosclerosis by agents that do not lower cholesterol.** *Br Heart J* 1993, **69**(suppl):S54–S62.

16. Deanfield J et al.: **Cigarette smoking and the treatment of angina with propranolol, atenolol, and nifedipine.** *N Engl J Med* 1984, **310**:951–954.

17. Fox K et al.: **Interaction between cigarettes and propranolol in treatment of angina pectoris.** *BMJ* 1980, **281**:191–193.

18. Aronow WS: **Aggravation of angina pectoris by two percent carboxyhemoglobin.** *Am Heart J* 1981, **101**:154–157.

19. Rennard S *et al.*: **Nicotine replacement therapy for patients with coronary artery disease.** *Arch Intern Med* 1994, **154**:989–995.

20. Gould KL: **Noninvasive assessment of coronary stenoses by myocardial perfusion imaging during pharmacologic coronary vasodilation. 1. Physiologic basis and experimental validation.** *Am J Cardiol* 1978, **41**:267–278.

21. Sacks HS *et al.*: **Dipyridamole in the treatment of angina pectoris: a meta-analysis.** *Thromb Res* 1990, **60**:35–42.

22. Crea F *et al.*: **Effect of theophylline on exercise-induced myocardial ischaemia.** *Lancet* 1989, **i**:683–686.

23. Crea F *et al.*: **Effects of theophylline, atenolol and their combination on myocardial ischemia in stable angina pectoris.** *Am J Cardiol* 1990, **66**:1157–1162.

24. Anversa P *et al.*: **Quantitative structural analysis of the myocardium during physiologic growth and induced cardiac hypertrophy: a review.** *J Am Coll Cardiol* 1986, **7**:1140–1149.

25. Meyer BJ, Amann FW: **Additional antianginal efficacy of amiodarone in patients with limiting angina pectoris.** *Am Heart J* 1993, **125**:996–1001.

26. Melandri G *et al.*: **Benefit of adding low molecular weight heparin to the conventional treatment of stable angina pectoris: a double-blind, randomized, placebo-controlled trial.** *Circulation* 1993, **88**:2517–2523.

27. Fujita M *et al.*: **Prospective, randomized, placebo-controlled, double-blind, multicenter study of exercise with enoxaparin pretreatment for stable-effort angina.** *Am Heart J* 1995, **129**:535–541.

28. Deanfield JE *et al.*: **Amlodipine reduces transient myocardial ischemia in patients with coronary artery disease: double-blind Circadian Anti-ischemia Program in Europe (CAPE trial).** *J Am Coll Cardiol* 1994, **24**:1460–1467.

29. Knatterud GL *et al.*: **Effects of treatment strategies to suppress ischemia in patients with coronary artery disease: 12-week results of the Asymptomatic Cardiac Ischemia Pilot (ACIP) study.** *J Am Coll Cardiol* 1994, **24**:11–20.

30. Von Arnim T: **Medical treatment to reduce total ischemic burden: Total Ischemic Burden Bisoprolol Study (TIBBS), a multicenter trial comparing bisoprolol and nifedipine.** *J Am Coll Cardiol* 1995, **251**:231–238.

31. Pepine CJ *et al.*: **Effects of treatment on outcome in mildly symptomatic patients with ischemia during daily life: the Atenolol Silent Ischemia Study (ASIST).** *Circulation* 1994, **90**:762–768.

32. Dargie HJ *et al.*: **Total Ischaemic Burden European Trial (TIBET): effects of ischaemia and treatment with atenolol, nifedipine SR and their combination on outcome in patients with chronic stable angina.** *Eur Heart J*, in press.

33. Fox *et al.*: **Total Ischaemic Burden European Trial (TIBET): effects of ischaemia and treatment with atenolol, nifedipine SR and their combination on the exercise test and the total ischaemic burden in 608 patients with stable angina.** *Eur Heart J*, in press.

34. Ardissiono D *et al.*: **Selection of medical treatment in stable angina pectoris: results of the International Multicenter Angina Exercise (IMAGE) study.** *J Am Coll Cardiol* 1995, **25**:1516–1521.

35. Rehnqvist N *et al.*: **Ventricular arrhythmias and other base-line data in 790 patients followed for angina pectoris. Prognostic value and therapeutic implications. Report from APSIS.** *New Trends Arrhythmias* 1993, **9**:1169–1173.

36. Parker JO *et al.*: **Intermittent transdermal nitroglycerin therapy in angina pectoris. Clinically effective without rebound or tolerance.** *Circulation* 1995, **91**:1368–1374.

37. Akhras F *et al.*: **Efficacy of intermittent (eight hours off) transdermal nitrate therapy in stable angina.** *Int J Cardiol* 1994, **43**:251–256.

38. De Milliano PA *et al.*: **Long-term efficacy of continuous and intermittent use of transdermal nitroglycerin in stable angina pectoris.** *Am J Cardiol* 1991, **68**:857–862.

39. Paciaroni E, Luca C: **Discontinuous transdermal nitroglycerin as treatment for stable angina in the elderly: a double-blind multicentre study.** *Eur Heart J* 1991, **12**:1076–1080.

40. DeMots H, Glasser SP: **Intermittent transdermal nitroglycerin therapy in the treatment of chronic stable angina.** *J Am Coll Cardiol* 1989, **13**:786–793.

41. Nordlander R *et al.*: **Once- versus twice-daily administration of controlled-release isosorbide-5-mononitrate 60 mg in the treatment of stable angina pectoris. A randomized, double-blind, cross-over study.** *Eur Heart J* 1994, **15**:108–113.

42. Thadani U *et al.*: **Lack of pharmacologic tolerance and rebound angina pectoris during twice-daily therapy with isosorbide-5-mononitrate.** *Ann Intern Med* 1994, **120**:353–359.

43. Parker JO: **Eccentric dosing with isosorbide-5-mononitrate in angina pectoris.** *Am J Cardiol* 1993, **72**:871–876.

44. Chrysant SG *et al.*: **Efficacy and safety of extended-release isosorbide mononitrate for stable effort angina pectoris.** *Am J Cardiol* 1993, **72**:1249–1256.

45. Aschermann M *et al.*: **Randomized double-blind comparison of isosorbide dinitrate and nifedipine in variant angina pectoris.** *Am J Cardiol* 1990, **65**:46J–49J.

46. Dargie H *et al.*: **Role of calcium antagonists in cardiovascular therapy.** *Br Heart J* 1981, **46**:8–16.

47. Findlay IN *et al.*: **Treatment of angina pectoris with nifedipine and atenolol: efficacy and effect on cardiac function.** *Br Heart J* 1986, **55**:240–245.

48. Yokota M *et al.*: **Duration and extent of antianginal effects of a sustained-release formulation of nifedipine in angina.** *Eur Heart J* 1994, **15**:965–970.

49. Parmley WW *et al.*: **Attenuation of the circadian patterns of myocardial ischemia with nifedipine GITS in patients with chronic stable angina.** *J Am Coll Cardiol* 1992, **19**:1380–1389.

50. Jaiprakash SS et al.: **Efficacy of nifedipine in the treatment of angina pectoris and chronic airways obstruction.** Postgrad Med J 1980, **56**:624–628.

51. Sklar J et al.: **Usefulness of nicarpadine as monotherapy for chronic, stable angina.** Am J Cardiol 1989, **63**:1203–1207.

52. Ezekowitz MD et al.: **Amlodipine in chronic stable angina: results of a multicenter double-blind crossover trial.** Am Heart J 1995, **129**:527–535.

53. DiBianco R et al.: **Amlodipine combined with beta blockade for chronic angina: results of a multicenter, placebo-controlled, randomized double-blind study.** Clin Cardiol 1992, **15**:519–524.

54. Taylor SH et al.: **A double-blind, placebo-controlled, parallel dose-response study of amlodipine in stable exertional angina pectoris.** J Cardiovasc Pharmacol 1991, **17**:S46–S49.

55. Mehta JL: **Emerging options in the management of myocardial ischaemia.** Am J Cardiol 1994, **73**:18A–27A.

56. Chahine RA et al.: **Randomized placebo-controlled trial of amlodipine in vasospastic angina.** J Am Coll Cardiol 1993, **21**:1365–1370.

57. Schulte KL: **24 h antianginal and anti-ischaemic effects with once daily felodipine. A double-blind comparison with nifedipine, twice daily, and placebo in patients with stable exercise induced angina pectoris.** Eur Heart J 1995, **16**:171–176.

58. Thadani U et al.: **Duration of effects of isradipine during twice daily therapy in angina pectoris.** Cardiovasc Drugs Ther 1994, **8**:199–210.

59. Glasser SP: **Nisoldipine coat core as concomitant therapy in chronic stable angina pectoris.** Am J Cardiol 1995, **75**:68E–70E.

60. Thadani U et al.: **Dose-response evaluation of once-daily therapy with a new formulation of diltiazem for stable angina pectoris.** Am J Cardiol 1994, **74**:9–17.

61. Stone PH et al.: **Comparison of propranolol, diltiazem, and nifedipine in the treatment of ambulatory ischemia in patients with stable angina. Differential effects on ambulatory ischemia, exercise performance, and anginal symptoms.** Circulation 1990, **82**:1962–1972.

62. Frances Y et al.: **Twenty-four hour efficacy of two dose levels of a once daily sustained-release diltiazem formulation in stable angina: a placebo-controlled trial.** Br J Clin Pharmacol 1995, 277–282.

63. Klinke WP et al.: **Usefulness of sustained-release diltiazem for stable angina pectoris.** Am J Cardiol 1989, **64**:1249–1252.

64. Go MJ, Hollenberg M: **Improved efficacy of high-dose versus medium- and low-dose diltiazem therapy for chronic stable angina pectoris.** Am J Cardiol 1984, **53**:669–673.

65. Weiner DA et al.: **The efficacy of safety of high-dose verapamil and diltiazem in the long-term treatment of stable exertional angina.** Clin Cardiol 1984, **7**:648–653.

66. Schroeder JS et al.: **Multiclinic controlled trial of diltiazem for Prinzmetal's angina.** Am J Med 1982, **72**:227–232.

67. Winniford MD et al.: **Propranolol-verapamil versus propranolol-nifedipine in severe angina pectoris of effort: a randomized, double-blind, crossover study.** Am J Cardiol 1985, **55**:281–285.

68. Findlay IN et al.: **A double-blind placebo controlled comparison of verapamil, atenolol, and their combination in patients with chronic stable angina pectoris.** Br Heart J 1987, **57**:336–343.

69. Winniford MD et al.: **Verapamil therapy for Prinzmetal's variant angina: comparison with placebo and nifedipine.** Am J Cardiol 1982, **50**:913–918.

70. Dorow P et al.: **Effects of single oral doses of bisoprolol and atenolol on airway function in nonasthmatic chronic obstructive lung disease and angina pectoris.** Eur J Clin Pharmacol 1986, **31**:143–147.

71. Boyle RM et al.: **A comparison of once and twice daily atenolol for angina pectoris.** Int J Cardiol 1983, **3**:25–35.

72. Solomon SA et al.: **A placebo-controlled, double-blind study of eicosapentaenoic acid-rich fish oil in patients with stable angina pectoris.** Curr Med Res Opin 1990, **12**:1–11.

73. Salachas A et al.: **Effects of a low-dose fish oil concentrate on angina, exercise tolerance time, serum triglycerides, and platelet function.** Angiology 1994, **45**:1023–1031.

74. Todd IC, Ballantyne D: **Effect of exercise training on the total ischaemic burden: an assessment by 24 hour ambulatory electrocardiographic monitoring.** Br Heart J 1992, **68**:560–566.

75. Todd IC et al.: **Effects of daily high-intensity exercise on myocardial perfusion in angina pectoris.** Am J Cardiol 1991, **68**:1593–1599.

76. Todd IC, Ballantyne D: **Antianginal efficacy of exercise training: a comparison with beta blockade.** Br Heart J 1990, **64**:14–19.

77. Rees Jones DI, Oliver IM: **A comparison of the antianginal efficacy of nifedipine alone and the fixed combination of atenolol and nifedipine.** Br J Clin Pract 1994, **48**:174–177.

78. Emanuelsson H et al.: **Felodipine versus placebo in stable effort-induced angina pectoris in patients inadequately controlled with metoprolol: a dose-finding study.** J Cardiovasc Pharmacol 1994, **24**:303–309.

79. Foale RA: **Atenolol versus the fixed combination of atenolol and nifedipine in stable angina pectoris.** Eur Heart J 1993, **14**:1369–1374.

80. Johnston DL et al.: **Clinical and hemodynamic evaluation of propranolol in combination with verapamil, nifedipine and diltiazem in exertional angina pectoris: a placebo-controlled, double-blind, randomized, crossover study.** Am J Cardiol 1985, **55**:680–687.

81. Subramanian VB et al.: **Combined therapy with verapamil and propranolol in chronic stable angina.** Am J Cardiol 1982, **49**:125–132.

82. De Caprio L et al.: **Acute effects of nifedipine, diltiazem and their combination in patients with chronic stable angina: a double-blind, randomized, cross-over, placebo-controlled study.** Eur Heart J 1993, **14**:416–420.

83. De Vries RJM et al.: Comparison between felodipine and isosorbide mononitrate as adjunct to beta blockade in patients >65 years of age with angina pectoris. Am J Cardiol 1994, 74:1201–1206.

84. Van de Ven LLM et al.: Which drug to choose for stable angina pectoris: a comparative study between bisoprolol and nitrates. Int J Cardiol 1995, 47:217–223.

85. Uberbacher HJ et al.: Randomised double-blind comparison of isosorbide-5-mononitrate and sustained release nifedipine in patients with stable exercise-induced angina. Drug Invest 1991, 3:210–219.

86. Raftery EB et al.: A double-blind comparison of a beta-blocker and a potassium channel opener in exercise induced angina. Eur Heart J 1993, 14:35–39.

87. Meeter K et al.: Efficacy of nicorandil versus propranolol in mild stable angina pectoris of effort: a long-term, double-blind, randomized study. J Cardiovasc Pharmacol 1992, 20:S59–S66.

88. Ulvenstam G et al.: Antianginal and anti-ischemic efficacy of nicorandil compared with nifedipine in patients with angina pectoris and coronary heart disease: a double-blind, randomized, multicenter study. J Cardiovasc Pharmacol 1992, 20:S67–S73.

89. DeWood MA, Wolbach RA: Randomized double-blind comparison of side effects of nicarpidine and nifedipine in angina pectoris. Am Heart J 1990, 119(suppl II):468–478.

90. Scardi S et al.: Efficacy of continuous and intermittent transdermal treatment with nitroglycerin in effort angina pectoris: a multicentre study. Int J Cardiol 1991, 32:241–248.

91. Siu SC et al.: Comparative efficacy of nifedipine gastrointestinal therapeutic system versus diltiazem when added to beta blockers in stable angina pectoris. Am J Cardiol 1993, 71:887–892.

92. Wallace WA et al.: Comparison of antianginal efficacies and exercise hemodynamic effects of nifedipine and diltiazem in stable angina pectoris. Am J Cardiol 1989, 63:414–418.

93. Bernink PJLM et al.: An 8-week double-blind study of amlodipine and diltiazem in patients with stable exertional angina pectoris. J Cardiovasc Pharmacol 1991, 17:S53–S56.

94. Foale RA, Vandenburg MJ: Sustained-release verapamil and nifedipine in exercise-induced angina pectoris. Eur Heart J 1992, 13:256–260.

95. Subramanian VB et al.: Randomized double-blind comparison of verapamil and nifedipine in chronic stable angina. Am J Cardiol 1982, 50:696–703.

96. Subramanian VB et al.: Rationale for the choice of calcium antagonists in chronic stable angina. An objective double-blind placebo-controlled comparison of nifedipine and verapamil. Am J Cardiol 1982, 50:1173–1179.

97. Wallace WA et al.: Comparison of nifedipine gastrointestinal therapeutic system and atenolol on antianginal efficacies and exercise hemodynamic responses in stable angina pectoris. Am J Cardiol 1994, 73:23–28.

98. Van der Does R et al.: Efficacy and safety of carvedilol in comparison with nifedipine sustained-release in chronic stable angina. J Cardiovasc Pharmacol 1992, 19:S122–S127.

99. Higginbotham MB et al.: Chronic stable angina monotherapy. Nifedipine versus propranolol. Am J Med 1989, 86:1–5.

100. Ardissino D et al.: Transient myocardial ischemia during daily life in rest and exertional angina pectoris and comparison of effectiveness of metoprolol versus nifedipine. Am J Cardiol 1991, 67:946–952.

101. Shapiro W et al.: Comparison of atenolol and nifedipine in chronic stable angina pectoris. Am J Cardiol 1989, 64:186–190.

102. Singh S: Long-term double-blind evaluation of amlodipine and nadolol in patients with stable exertional angina pectoris. Clin Cardiol 1993, 16:54–58.

103. Posma JL et al.: Sustained-release diltiazem versus metoprolol in stable angina pectoris. Eur Heart J 1989, 10:923–927.

104. Hopkinson ND et al.: A comparison of sustained release verapamil versus atenolol for 24 h protection from exercise-induced angina. Eur Heart J 1991, 12:1273–1277.

105. Bowles MJ et al.: Double-blind randomized crossover trial of verapamil and propranolol in chronic stable angina. Am J Cardiol 1983, 106:1297–1306.

106. Frishman WH et al.: Superiority of verapamil to propranolol in stable angina pectoris: a double-blind, randomized crossover trial. Circulation 1982, 65:I-51–I-59.

107. Ray SG et al.: Cardiorespiratory and symptomatic variables during maximal and submaximal exercise in men with stable effort angina: a comparison of atenolol and celiprolol. Eur Heart J 1994, 15:1566–1570.

108. De Muinck ED et al.: Comparison of the safety and efficacy of bisoprolol versus atenolol in stable exercise-induced angina pectoris: a Multicenter International Randomized Study of Angina Pectoris (MIRSA). J Cardiovasc Pharmacol 1992, 19:870–875.

109. Frishman WH et al.: Comparison of celiprolol and propranolol in stable angina pectoris. Am J Cardiol 1991, 67:665–670.

110. Meyer TE et al.: Comparison of the efficacy of atenolol and its combination with slow-release nifedipine in chronic stable angina. Cardiovasc Drugs Ther 1993, 7:909–913.

111. Parameshwar J et al.: Atenolol or nicardipine alone is as efficacious in stable angina as their combination: a double blind randomised trial. Int J Cardiol 1993, 40:135–141.

112. Vlay SC, Olson LC: Nifedipine and isosorbide dinitrate alone and in combination for patients with chronic stable angina: a double-blind crossover study. Am Heart J 1990, 120:303–307.

113. Peart I et al.: Cold intolerance in patients with angina pectoris: effect of nifedipine and propranolol. Br Heart J 1989, 61:521–528.

114. Akhras F, Jackson G: Efficacy of nifedipine and isosorbide mononitrate in combination with atenolol in stable angina. Lancet 1991, 338:1036–1039.

115. Clelend J, McMurray J, Ray S (eds): *Prevention Strategies after Myocardial Infarction.* London: Science Press; 1994.

116. Opie LH *et al.*: **Nifedipine and mortality: grave defects in the dossier.** *Circulation* 1995, **92**:1068–1073.

117. Lichtlen PR *et al.*: **Retardation of angiographic progression of coronary artery disease by nifedipine. Results of the International Nifedipine Trial on Antiatherosclerotic Therapy (INTACT).** *Lancet* 1990, **335**:1109–1113.

118. Waters D *et al.*: **A controlled clinical trial to assess the effect of a calcium channel blocker on the progression of coronary atherosclerosis.** *Circulation* 1990, **82**:1940–1953.

119. Furberg CD *et al.*: **Nifedipine: dose-related increase in mortality in patients with coronary heart disease.** *Circulation* 1995, **92**:1326–1331.

120. Yusuf S: **Calcium antagonists in coronary artery disease and hypertension: time for revaluation?** *Circulation* 1995, **92**:1079–1082.

121. Kloner RA: **Nifedipine in ischemic heart disease.** *Circulation* 1995, **92**:1074–1078.

122. O'Keefe JH *et al.*: **Effects of diltiazem on complications and restenosis after coronary angioplasty.** *Am J Cardiol* 1991, **67**:373–376.

123. Serruys PW *et al.*: **Does the new angiotensin converting enzyme inhibitor cilazapril prevent restenosis after percutaneous transluminal coronary angioplasty? Results of the MERCATOR study: a multicenter, randomized, double-blind placebo-controlled trial.** *Circulation* 1992, **86**:100–110.

124. Faxon DP *et al.*: **Effect of high dose angiotensin-converting enzyme inhibition on restenosis: final results of the MARCATOR study, a multicenter, double-blind, placebo-controlled trial of cilazapril.** *J Am Coll Cardiol* 1995, **25**:362–369.

125. Yusuf S *et al.*: **Effect of enalapril on myocardial infarction and unstable angina in patients with low ejection fractions.** *Lancet* 1992, **340**:1173–1178.

126. Cleland JG: **ACE inhibitors for the prevention and treatment of heart failure: insights from the SOLVD trials.** *Eur Heart J* 1994, **15**:125–130.

127. Texter M *et al.*: **The Quinapril Ischaemic Event Trial (QUIET) design and methods: evaluation of chronic ACE inhibitor therapy after coronary artery intervention.** *Cardiovasc Drugs Ther* 1993, **7**:273–282.

128. Timmis AD: **Will serum enzymes and other proteins find a clinical application in the early diagnosis of myocardial infarction?** *Br Heart J* 1994, **71**:309–310.

129. Walldius G *et al.*: **The effect of probucol on femoral atherosclerosis: the Probucol Quantitative Regression Swedish Trial (PQRST).** *Am J Cardiol* 1994, **74**:875–883.

130. Gapinski JP *et al.*: **Preventing restenosis with fish oils following coronary angioplasty: a meta-analysis.** *Arch Intern Med* 1993, **153**:1595–1601.

131. The Alpha-Tocopherol, Beta Carotene Cancer Prevention Study Group.The effect of vitamin E and beta carotene on the incidence of lung cancer and other cancers in male smokers. *N Engl J Med* 1994, **330**:1029–1035.

132. Blot WJ *et al.*: **Nutrition intervention trials in Linxian, China: supplementation with specific vitamin/mineral combinations, cancer incidence, and disease-specific mortality in the general population.** *J Natl Cancer Inst* 1993, **85**:1483–1492.

133. Stephens NG *et al.*: **CHAOS: a controlled trial of vitamin E in patients with ischaemic heart disease: interim report of effects on cardiovascular events.** *Eur Heart J* 1995, **16**(suppl):20.

134. Gaziano JM *et al.*: **Beta-carotene therapy for chronic stable angina [Abstract].** *Circulation* 1990, **82**(suppl III):201.

135. Manson JE *et al.*: **Aspirin in the primary prevention of angina pectoris in a randomized trial of United States physicians.** *Am J Med* 1990, **89**:772–776.

136. Steering Committee of the Physicians' Health Study Research Group: **Final report on the aspirin component of the ongoing Physicians' Health Study.** *N Engl J Med* 1989, **321**:129–135.

137. Borchgrevink CF: **Long-term anticoagulant therapy in angina pectoris.** *Lancet* 1962, **i**:449–451.

138. Chesebro JH *et al.*: **Antiplatelet therapy in coronary disease progression: reduced infarction and new lesion formation [Abstract].** *Circulation* 1989, **80**(suppl II):266.

139. Jull Moller S *et al.*: **Double-blind trial of aspirin in primary prevention of myocardial infarction in patients with stable chronic angina pectoris.** *Lancet* 1992, **340**:1421–1425.

140. Ridker PM *et al.*: **Low-dose aspirin therapy for chronic stable angina. A randomized, placebo-controlled trial.** *Ann Intern Med* 1991, **114**:835–839.

141. Peto R *et al.*: **Randomised trial of prophylactic daily aspirin in British male doctors.** *BMJ* 1988, **296**:313–316.

142. Brooks N *et al.*: **Randomised placebo controlled trial of aspirin and dipyridamole in the prevention of coronary vein graft occlusion.** *Br Heart J* 1985, **53**:201–207.

143. Gerschlick AH *et al.*: **Long term clinical outcome of coronary surgery and assessment of the benefit obtained with postoperative aspirin and dipyridamole.** *Br Heart J* 1988, **60**:111–116.

144. Chesebro JH *et al.*: **Effect of dipyridamole and aspirin on late vein-graft patency after coronary bypass operations.** *N Engl J Med* 1984, **310**:209–214.

145. Goldman S *et al.*: **Improvement in early saphenous vein graft patency after coronary artery bypass surgery with antiplatelet therapy: results of a Veterans Administration Cooperative Study.** *Circulation* 1988, **77**:1324–1332.

146. Goldman S *et al.*: **Long-term graft patency (3 years) after coronary artery surgery: effects of aspirin. Results of a VA cooperative study.** *Circulation* 1994, **89**:1138–1143.

147. Van der Meer J *et al.*: **Prevention of one-year vein-graft occlusion after aortocoronary-bypass surgery: a comparison of low-dose aspirin, low-dose aspirin plus dipyridamole, and oral anticoagulants.** *Lancet* 1993, **342**:257–264.

148. Pfisterer M et al.: **Trial of low-dose aspirin plus dipyridamole versus anticoagulants for prevention of aortocoronary vein graft occlusion.** Lancet 1989, **ii**: 1–7.

149. Cleland JGF et al.: **Effect of coronary artery bypass graft surgery on survival [1].** Lancet 1994, **344**:1222–1224.

150. Hjermann I et al.: **Effect of diet and smoking intervention on the incidence of coronary heart disease. Report from the Oslo Study Group of a randomised trial in healthy men.** Lancet 1981, **2**:1303–1310.

151. Multiple Risk Factor Intervention Trial Research Group: **Risk factor changes and mortality results.** JAMA 1982, **248**:1465–1477.

152. Multiple Risk Factor Intervention Trial Research Group: **Mortality rates after 10.5 years for participants in the multiple risk factor intervention trial. Findings related to a priori hypotheses of the trial.** JAMA 1990, **263**:1795–1801.

153. Multiple Risk Factor Intervention Trial Research Group: **Exercise electrocardiogram and coronary heart disease mortality in the multiple risk factor intervention trial.** Am J Cardiol 1985, **55**:16–24.

154. Rose G on behalf of the WHO Collaborative Group: **European collaborative trial of multifactorial prevention of coronary heart disease.** Lancet 1986, **i**:869–872.

155. World Health Organization European Collaborative Group: **Multifactorial trial in the prevention of coronary heart disease: 3. Incidence and mortality results.** Eur Heart J 1983, **4**:141–147.

156. World Health Organization European Collaborative Group: **European collaborative trial of multifactorial prevention of coronary heart disease: final report on the 6-year results.** Lancet 1986, **i**:869–872.

157. Miettinen TA et al.: **Multifactorial primary prevention of cardiovascular diseases in middle-aged men. Risk factor changes, incidence, and mortality.** JAMA 1985, **254**:2097–2102.

158. Schuler G et al.: **Low-fat diet and regular, supervised physical exercise in patients with symptomatic coronary artery disease: reduction of stress-induced myocardial ischaemia.** Circulation 1988, **77**:172–181.

159. Schuler G et al.: **Regular physical exercise and low-fat diet. Effects on progression of coronary artery disease.** Circulation 1992, **86**:1–11.

160. Haskell WL et al.: **Effects of intensive multiple risk factor reduction on coronary atherosclerosis and clinical cardiac events in men and women with coronary artery disease: the Stanford Coronary Risk Intervention Project (SCRIP).** Circulation 1994, **89**:975–990.

161. Medical Research Council Working Party: **MRC trial of treatment of mild hypertension: principal results.** BMJ 1985, **291**:97–102.

162. European Working Party on High Blood Pressure in the Elderly: **Mortality and morbidity results from the European working party on high blood pressure in the elderly trial.** Lancet 1985, **i**:1349–1354.

163. Coope J, Warrender TS: **Randomised trial of treatment of hypertension in elderly patients in primary care.** BMJ 1986, **293**:1145–1151.

164. Collins R et al.: **Blood pressure, stroke, and coronary heart disease. Part 2, short-term reductions in blood pressure: overview of randomised drug trials in their epidemiological context.** Lancet 1990, **335**:827–838.

165. SHEP Cooperative Research Group: **Prevention of stroke by antihypertensive drug treatment in older persons with isolated systolic hypertension. Final results of the Systolic Hypertension in the Elderly Program (SHEP).** JAMA 1991, **265**:3255–3264.

166. Meade TW, Miller GJ: **Combined use of aspirin and warfarin in primary prevention of ischemic heart disease in men at high risk.** Am J Cardiol 1995, **75**: 23B–26B.

167. Dahlöf B et al.: **Morbidity and mortality in the Swedish Trial in Old Patients with Hypertension (STOP-Hypertension).** Lancet 1991, **388**:1281–1285.

168. Dorr AE et al.: **Colestipol hydrochloride in hypercholesterolaemic patients: effect on serum cholesterol and mortality.** J Chron Dis 1978, **31**:5–14.

169. Brensike JF et al.: **Effects of therapy with cholestyramine on progression of coronary arteriosclerosis: results of the NHLBI Type II Coronary Intervention Study.** Circulation 1984, **69**:313–324.

170. Cashin-Hamphill L et al.: **Beneficial effects of colestipol-niacin on coronary atherosclerosis. A 4-year follow-up.** JAMA 1990, **264**:3013–3017.

171. Blankenhorn DH et al.: **Beneficial effects of combined colestipol-niacin therapy on coronary atherosclerosis and coronary venous bypass grafts.** JAMA 1987, **257**:3233–3240.

172. Brown G et al.: **Regression of coronary artery disease as a result of intensive lipid-lowering therapy in men with high levels of apolipoprotein B.** N Engl J Med 1990, **323**:1289–1298.

173. Watts GF et al.: **Effects on coronary artery disease of lipid-lowering diet, or diet plus cholestyramine, in the St Thomas' Atherosclerosis Regression Study (STARS).** Lancet 1992, **339**:563–569.

174. Research Committee of the Scottish Society of Physicians: **Ischaemic Heart Disease. A secondary prevention trial using clofibrate.** BMJ 1971, **4**:775–784.

175. Group of Physicians of the Newcastle upon Tyne Region: **Trial of clofibrate in the treatment of ischaemic heart disease.** BMJ 1971, **4**:767–775.

176. Oliver MF et al.: **A co-operative trial in the prevention of ischaemic heart disease using clofibrate. Report from the Committee of Principal Investigators.** Br Heart J 1978, **40**:1069–1118.

177. Frick MH et al.: **Helsinki Heart Study: primary-prevention trial with gemfibrozil in middle-aged men with dyslipidemia. Safety of treatment, changes in risk factors, and incidence of coronary heart disease.** N Engl J Med 1987, **317**:1237–1245.

178. Feher MD et al.: **Long term safety of statin-fibrate combination treatment in the management of hypercholesterolaemia in patients with coronary artery disease.** Br Heart J 1995, **74**:14–17.

179. Shepherd J: **Fibrates and statins in the treatment of hyperlipidaemia: an appraisal of their efficacy and safety.** Eur Heart J 1995, **16**:5–13.

180. Furberg CD et al.: **Effect of lovastatin on early carotid atherosclerosis and cardiovascular events. Asymptomatic Carotid Artery Progression Study (ACAPS) Research Group.** Circulation 1994, **90**: 1679–1687.

181. The Pravastatin Multinational Study Group for Cardiac Risk Patients: **Effects of pravastatin in patients with serum total cholesterol levels from 5.2 to 7.8 mmol/liter (200 to 300 mg/dl) plus two additional atherosclerotic risk factors.** Am J Cardiol 1993, **72**:1031–1037.

182. Jukema JW et al.: **Effects of lipid lowering by pravastatin on progression and regression of coronary artery disease in symptomatic men with normal to moderately elevated serum cholesterol levels. The Regression Growth Evaluation Statin Study (REGRESS).** Circulation 1995, **91**:2520–2540.

183. Bradford RH et al.: **Expanded Clinical Evaluation of Lovastatin (EXCEL) study results: two-year efficacy and safety follow-up.** Am J Cardiol 1994, **74**:667– 673.

184. Pedersen TR: **Randomised trial of cholesterol lowering in 4444 patients with coronary heart disease: the Scandinavian Simvastatin Survival Study (4S).** Lancet 1994, **344**:1383–1389.

185. Cleland JGF: Unpublished data, 1996.

186. Shepherd MD et al.: **Prevention of coronary heart disease with pravastatin in men with hypercholesterolaemia.** N Engl J Med 1995, **333**: 1301–1307

187. Pitt B et al.: **Design and recruitment in the United States of a multicenter quantitative angiographic trial of pravastatin to limit atherosclerosis in the coronary arteries (PLAC I).** Am J Cardiol 1993, **72**:31–35.

188. Blankenhorn DH et al.: **Coronary angiographic changes with lovastatin therapy: the Monitored Atherosclerosis Regression Study (MARS).** Ann Intern Med 1993, **119**:969–976.

189. Waters D et al.: **Effects of monotherapy with an HMG-CoA reductase inhibitor on the progression of coronary atherosclerosis as assessed by serial quantitative arteriography: the Canadian Coronary Atherosclerosis Intervention Trial.** Circulation 1994, **89**:959–968.

190. Simoons ML et al.: **Effect of simvastatin on coronary atheroma: the Multicentre Anti-Atheroma Study (MAAS).** Lancet 1994, **344**:633–638.

191. Cleland JGF: **Beta-blocking agents in heart failure. Should they be used and how?** Eur Heart J 1995, in press.

192. Holme I: **An analysis of randomized trials evaluating the effect of cholesterol reduction on total mortality and coronary heart disease incidence.** Circulation 1990, **82**:1916–1924.

193. The VA Coronary Artery Bypass Surgery Cooperative Study Group: **Eighteen-year follow-up in the Veterans Affairs Cooperative Study of Coronary Artery Bypass Surgery for Stable Angina.** Circulation 1992, **86**:121–130.

194. The Veterans Administration Coronary Artery Bypass Surgery Cooperative Study Group: **Eleven-year survival in the Veterans Administration randomized trial of coronary bypass surgery for stable angina.** N Engl J Med 1984, **311**:1333–1339.

195. Hultgren HN et al.: **The 5 year effect of bypass surgery on relief of angina and exercise performance.** Circulation 1985, **72(suppl V)**:V-79–V-83.

196. Peduzzi P et al.: **Ten-year incidence of myocardial infarction and prognosis after infarction.** Circulation 1991, **83**:747–755.

197. European Coronary Surgery Study Group: **Survival, myocardial infarction, and employment status in a prospective randomized study of coronary bypass surgery.** Circulation 1985, **72(suppl V)**:V-90–V-101.

198. European Coronary Surgery Study Group: **Twelve-year follow-up of survival in the randomized European Coronary Surgery Study.** N Engl J Med 1988, **319**:332–337.

199. European Coronary Surgery Study Group: **Long-term results of prospective randomised study of coronary artery bypass surgery in stable angina pectoris.** Lancet 1982, i8309–8312.

200. CASS Principal Investigators: **Coronary Artery Surgery Study (CASS): a randomized trial of coronary artery bypass surgery. Survival data.** Circulation 1983, **68**:939–950.

201. CASS Principal Investigators: **Coronary artery Surgery Study (CASS): a randomized trial of coronary artery bypass surgery. Quality of life in patients randomly assigned to treatment groups.** Circulation 1983, **68**:951–960.

202. CASS Principal Investigators: **Myocardial infarction and mortality in the Coronary Artery Surgery Study (CASS) randomized trial.** N Engl J Med 1984, **310**:750–758.

203. Yusuf S et al.: **Effect of coronary artery bypass graft surgery on survival: overview of 10-year results from randomised trials by the Coronary Artery Bypass Graft Surgery Trialists Collaboration.** Lancet 1994, **344**:563–570.

204. Gersh BJ et al.: **Comparison of coronary artery bypass surgery and medical therapy in patients 65 years of age or older. A nonrandomized study from the Coronary Artery Surgery Study (CASS) registry.** N Engl J Med 1985, **313**:217–224.

205. Parisi AF et al.: **A comparison of angioplasty with medical therapy in the treatment of single-vessel coronary artery disease.** N Engl J Med 1992, **326**:10–16.

206. Hampton JR et al.: **Coronary angioplasty versus coronary artery bypass surgery: the Randomised Intervention Treatment of Angina (RITA) trial.** Lancet 1993, **341**:573–580.

207. Hamm CW et al.: **A randomized study of coronary angioplasty compared with bypass surgery in patients with symptomatic multivessel coronary disease.** N Engl J Med 1994, **331**:1037–1043.

208. King SBII et al.: **A randomized trial comparing coronary angioplasty with coronary bypass surgery.** N Engl J Med 1994, **331**:1044–1050.

209. Goy J et al.: **Coronary angioplasty versus left internal mammary artery grafting for isolated proximal left anterior descending artery stenosis.** Lancet 1994, **343**:1449–1453.

210. CABRI Trial Participants: **First-year results of CABRI (Coronary Angioplasty versus Bypass Revascularisation Investigation).** Lancet 1995, **346**: 1179–1184.

211. Pocock SJ et al.: **Meta-analysis of randomised trials comparing coronary angioplasty with bypass surgery.** Lancet 1995, **346**:1184–1189.

212. Serruys PW et al.: **A comparison of balloon-expandable-stent implantation with balloon angioplasty in patients with coronary artery disease.** N Engl J Med 1994, **331**:489–495.

213. Fischman DL et al.: **A randomized comparison of coronary-stent placement and balloon angioplasty in the treatment of coronary artery disease.** N Engl J Med 1994, **331**:496–501.

214. Adelman AG et al.: **A comparison of directional atherectomy with balloon angioplasty for lesions of the left anterior descending coronary artery.** N Engl J Med 1993, **329**:228–233.

215. Topol EJ et al.: **A comparison of directional atherectomy with coronary angioplasty in patients with coronary artery disease.** N Engl J Med 1993, **329**:221–227.

216. Boehrer JD et al.: **Directional atherectomy versus ballon angioplasty for coronary ostial and nonostial left anterior descending coronary artery lesions results from a randomized multicenter trial. The CAVEAT-1 Investigators. Coronary Angioplasty Versus Excisional Atherectomy Trial.** J Am Coll Cardiol 1995, **25**:1380–1386.

217. Holmes DR et al.: **A multicenter, randomized trial of coronary angioplasty versus directional atherectomy for patients with saphenous vein bypass graft lesions. CAVEAT II Investigators.** Circulation 1995, **91**:1966–1974.

218. Jollis JG et al.: **The relation between the volume of coronary angioplasty procedures at hospitals treating Medicare beneficiaries and short-term mortality.** N Engl J Med 1994, **331**:1625–1629.

219. Cleland JGF: **Angioplasty versus medical therapy for single-vessel coronary artery disease** [Letter]. N Engl J Med 1992, **326**:1632–1634.

220. Schwartz L et al.: **Aspirin and dipyridamole in the prevention of restenosis after percutaneous transluminal coronary angioplasty.** N Engl J Med 1988, **318**:1714–1719.

221. Topol EJ et al.: **Randomised trial of coronary intervention with antibody against platelet IIb/IIIa integrin for reduction of clinical restenosis: results at six months.** Lancet 1994, **343**:881–886.

222. Tcheng JE et al.: **Pharmacodynamics of chimeric glycoprotein IIb/IIIa integrin antiplatlet antibody Fab 7E3 in high-risk coronary angioplasty.** Circulation 1994, **90**:1757–1764.

223. Ellis SG et al.: **Effect of 18- to 24-hour heparin administration for prevention of restenosis after uncomplicated coronary angioplasty.** Am Heart J 1989, **117**:777–782.

224. Faxon DR et al.: **Low molecular weight heparin in prevention of restenosis angioplasty. Results of Enoxaparin Restenosis (ERA) Trial.** Circulation 1994, **90**:908–914.

225. Urban P et al.: **Lack of effect of warfarin on the restenosis rate or on clinical outcome after balloon coronary angioplasty.** Br Heart J 1988, **60**:485–488.

226. Gershlick AH et al.: **Failure of epoprostenol (prostacyclin, PGI-2) to inhibit platelet aggregation and to prevent restenosis after coronary angioplasty: results of a randomised placebo controlled trial.** Br Heart J 1994, **71**:7–15.

227. Hillegass WB et al.: **A meta-analysis of randomized trials of calcium antagonists to reduce restenosis after coronary angioplasty.** Am J Cardiol 1994, **73**:835–839.

228. Weintraub WS et al.: **Lack of effect of lovastatin on restenosis after coronary angioplasty.** N Engl J Med 1994, **331**:1331–1337.

229. Braunwald E et al.: **Diagnosing and managing unstable angina.** Circulation 1994, **90**:613–622.

230. Narang R, Cleland J: **Current management of unstable angina.** Care of the Critically Ill 1994, **10**:252–257.

231. Telford AM, Wilson C: **Trial of heparin versus atenolol in prevention of myocardial infarction in intermediate coronary syndrome.** Lancet 1981, **i**: 1225–1228.

232. Lewis HD et al.: **Protective effects of aspirin against acute myocardial infarction and death in men with unstable angina. Results of a Veterans Administration Cooperative Study.** N Engl J Med 1983, **309**:396–403.

233. Cairns JA et al.: **Aspirin, sulfinpyrazone, or both in unstable angina. Results of a Canadian Multicenter Trial.** N Engl J Med 1985, **313**:1369–1375.

234. Theroux P et al.: **Aspirin, heparin, or both to treat acute unstable angina.** N Engl J Med 1988, **319**:1105–1111.

235. Theroux P et al.: **Reactivation of unstable angina after the discontinuation of heparin.** N Engl J Med 1992, **327**:141–145.

236. Neri–Serneri GG et al.: **Effect of heparin, aspirin, or alteplase in reduction of myocardial ischaemia in refractory unstable angina.** Lancet 1990, **335**:615–618.

237. Neri–Serneri GG et al.: **Randomised comparison of subcutaneous heparin, intravenous heparin, and aspirin in unstable angina. Studio Epoorine Sotto-cutanea nell'Angina Instabile (SESAIR) Refrattorie Group.** Lancet 1995, **345**:1201–1204.

238. Wallentin L: **Risk of myocardial infarction and death during treatment with low dose aspirin and intravenous heparin in men with unstable coronary artery disease.** Lancet 1990, **336**:827–830.

239. Nyman I et al.: **Prevention of serious cardiac events by low-dose aspirin in patient with silent myocardial ischaemia.** Lancet 1992, **340**:497–501.

240. Simoons ML et al.: **Randomized trial of a GPIIb/IIIa platelet receptor blocker in refractory unstable angina.** Circulation 1994, **89**:596–603.

241. Serruys PW et al. on behalf of the Helvetica Investigators: **A comparison of hirudin with heparin**

in the prevention of restenosis after coronary angioplasty. *N Engl J Med* 1995, **333**:757–763.

242. ISIS 2 (Second International Study of Infarct Survival) Collaborative Group: **Randomised trial of intravenous streptokinase, oral aspirin, both, or neither among 17,187 cases of suspected acute myocardial infarction: ISIS 2.** *Lancet* 1988, **ii**:349–360.

243. Gerstenblith G *et al.*: **Nifedipine in unstable angina. A double-blind, randomized trial.** *N Engl J Med* 1982, **306**:885–889.

244. Andre Fouet X *et al.*: **Comparison of short-term efficacy of diltiazem and propranolol in unstable angina at rest. A randomized trial in 70 patients.** *Eur Heart J* 1983, **4**:691–698.

245. Muller JE *et al.*: **Nifedipine and conventional therapy for unstable angina pectoris: a randomized, double-blind comparison.** *Circulation* 1984, **69**:728–739.

246. Theroux P *et al.*: **A randomized study comparing propranolol and diltiazem in the treatment of unstable angina.** *J Am Coll Cardiol* 1985, **5**:717–722.

247. The HINT research group: **Early treatment of unstable angina in the coronary care unit: a randomized, double-blind placebo-controlled comparison of recurrent ischaemia in patients treated with nifedipine or metoprolol or both.** *Br Heart J* 1986, **56**:400–413.

248. Hohnloser SH *et al.*: **Usefulness of esmolol in unstable angina pectoris.** *Am J Cardiol* 1991, **67**:1319–1323.

249. Held PH *et al.*: **Calcium channel blockers in acute myocardial infarction and unstable angina: an overview.** *BMJ* 1989, **299**:1187–1192.

250. Capucci A *et al.*: **Propranolol v. verapamil in the treatment of unstable angina. A double-blind crossover study.** *Eur Heart J* 1983, **4**:148–154.

251. Rizzon P *et al.*: **Randomized placebo-controlled comparative study of nifedipine, verapamil and isosorbide dinitrate in the treatment of angina at rest.** *Eur Heart J* 1986, **7**:67–76.

252. Myers MG *et al.*: **Nifedipine verus propranolol treatment for unstable angina in the elderly.** *Can J Cardiol* 1988, **4**:402–406.

253. Selden R *et al.*: **Medical versus surgical therapy for acute coronary insufficiency. A randomized study.** *N Engl J Med* 1975, **293**:1329–1333.

254. Pugh B *et al.*: **Unstable angina pectoris: a randomized study of patients treated medically and surgically.** *Am J Cardiol* 1978, **41**:1291–1298.

255. Russell RO *et al.*: **Unstable angina pectoris: national cooperative study group to compare surgical and medical therapy. II. In-hospital experience and initial follow-up results in patients with one, two and three vessel disease.** *Am J Cardiol* 1978, **42**:839–848.

256. Luchi RJ *et al.*: **Comparison of medical and surgical treatment for unstable angina pectoris. Results of a Veterans Administration cooperative study.** *N Engl J Med* 1987, **316**:977–984.

257. The TIMI IIIB investigators: **Effects of tissue plasminogen activator and a comparison of early invasive and conservative strategies in unstable angina and non-Q-wave myocardial infarction: results of the TIMI IIIB Trial. Thrombolysis in Myocardial Ischaemia.** *Circulation* 1994, **89**:1545–1556.

258. Sharma GVRK *et al.*: **Coronary bypass surgery improves survival in high-risk unstable angina. Results of a Veterans Administration cooperative study with an 8-year follow-up.** *Circulation* 1991, **84(suppl III)**:III-260–III-267.

259. Booth DC *et al.*: **Quality of life after bypass surgery for unstable angina. 5-year follow-up results of a veterans affairs cooperative study.** *Circulation* 1991, **83**:87–95.

260. Waters D, Lam JY: **Is thrombolytic therapy striking out in unstable angina [Editorial]?** *Circulation* 1992, **86**:1642–1644.

261. Ambrose JA *et al.*: **Adjunctive thrombolytic therapy during angioplasty for ischaemic rest angina: Results of the TAUSA trial.** *Circulation* 1994, **90**:69–77.

Management of chronic stable angina

Introduction

Most patients with coronary artery disease do not have angina and some patients with angina do not have coronary artery disease. Most patients with angina have myocardial ischaemia but some patients with myocardial ischaemia do not have angina.

The management of patients with suspected angina or with coronary disease will never be simple. However, because the object of management is to improve patient outcome, a few simple facts that help the decision-making process should be considered.

Prognosis

About 96% of patients with stable angina pectoris and 85% of those hospitalized with an episode of unstable angina will not have died or had MI after 1 year of follow-up. Of those with new-onset angina, about 90% will not have suffered infarction or death within 1 year. Although the rather favourable short to medium term prognosis of the great majority of patients with angina should be kept in mind, this is not grounds for complacency or inaction.

Any intervention must be low risk if it is to be widely deployed. Alternatively, innocuous tests that identify high-risk subsets can be used to identify patients in whom the risk of more aggressive intervention is warranted.

Angiography and revascularization

Coronary bypass surgery has not been shown to reduce the overall risk of MI, the frequency of perioperative infarction balancing the trend to later reduction in infarction. This is true for both stable and unstable angina. PTCA has not been shown to alter mortality, compared with surgery or medical therapy.

No evidence supports the use of angiography to determine the risk of MI in the hope of preventing it by coronary intervention. The coronary angiogram, as currently interpreted, is a poor predictor of which coronary lesions will occlude or cause infarction [1–4].

Angiography is not superior to clinical history (severity of symptoms) or an exercise test in determining who will benefit from surgery [5]. No evidence supports the use of routine angiography to determine whether a patient should undergo coronary intervention.

Coronary bypass surgery is associated with a high operative mortality in women and patients over 65 years of age [6,7]. There are no controlled trials to suggest that revascularization alters prognosis in these groups.

Indeed, despite advances in surgery the 30 day mortality for nonemergency CABG remains around 5% (average age 69 years) in the USA with a 1 year mortality of around 10% in the general population and 17% among higher risk patients [6,7].

Patients with asymptomatic myocardial ischaemia have not been shown to benefit prognostically from revascularization.

Over a 5-year period, a policy of surgery versus initial medical therapy (with surgery only for intractable symptoms) for stable angina saves about 10 lives for every 100 operations in those with three-vessel disease, 15 lives in those with left ventricular dysfunction and 13 lives in those with severe angina.

Data on symptoms and left ventricular dysfunction may be obtained noninvasively. The need for coronary arteriography for prognostic stratification is unproven. With the recent improvements in medical therapy, it is not clear whether surgery offers a decisive improvement in prognosis to any subgroup [8]. It is still perfectly reasonable to reserve surgery for those with symptoms that fail to respond adequately, in the patient's opinion, to medical therapy and who have important coronary artery disease in the doctor's opinion.

Angioplasty has not been shown to reduce the risk of infarction or death in stable or unstable angina, compared with medical therapy.

Managing coronary disease versus angina

Some medical treatments have been shown to be effective for the management of coronary atheroma, whereas others are effective for angina. Most patients with angina require treatment of both problems.

Diagnosis

An accurate diagnosis of angina pectoris is desirable in all patients but especially in younger patients whose employment, mortgage and life insurance will be affected by the diagnosis.

A highly abnormal ECG with no history of MI should alert the clinician to the possibility of other factors that may cause or exacerbate angina. These are shown in Figure 6.1; differential diagnosis of stable angina is shown in Figure 6.2. The classic criteria of angina are shown in Figure 3.1 (p. 29).

Patients without previous evidence of coronary disease

Clinical history is the single most powerful predictor of coronary disease in men: investigation adds little to the diagnosis in those with typical or atypical symptoms (see Appendix I and II). Further investigation should be carried out in men with equivocal symptoms. A man who can exercise adequately without untoward symptoms and who has a normal ECG is no more likely to have a coronary event than an asymptomatic patient. Those with at least 1.5 mm horizontal or downsloping ST-segment depression during exercise and suggestive symptoms almost certainly have coronary disease. An appropriate symptomatic response to medical therapy reinforces the diagnosis.

If the exercise test is equivocal, a trial of therapy may be instituted. The diagnosis should be reappraised in the light of the response to medical therapy. If doubt remains, then, on balance, a coronary angiogram is probably the quickest, least expensive, most

Fig. 6.1. *Causes of angina.*

Site	Specific cause
Coronary	Atherosclerosis Variation in coronary tone Thrombus
Left ventricular hypertrophy	Aortic stenosis Cardiomyopathy Hypertension (rarely sole cause of angina)
Right ventricular hypertrophy	Primary pulmonary hypertension Secondary pulmonary hypertension (mitral disease, cor pulmonale) Pulmonary stenosis
Tachycardia	Atrial fibrillation Thyrotoxicosis
Decreased blood oxygen content	Anaemia

Fig. 6.2. *Differential diagnosis of chronic stable angina.*

System	Diagnosis
Gastrointestinal	Reflux oesphagitis Peptic ulcer Cholecystitis
Chest wall	Various poorly defined entities

generally available and most accurate way of determining if coronary disease is present, although the presence of coronary disease does not necessarily mean that the patient has angina. However, if facilities for stress imaging are readily available (and known to be of high quality from internal audit), this can be used as an alternative method of investigation.

The relationship between coronary artery disease, symptoms and ischaemia should be confirmed by stress imaging in patients with atypical symptoms, before revascularization.

The diagnosis of angina by history in women is more difficult: noninvasive tests are less accurate and the prevalence of angina below the age of 60 years is much lower than in men (see Appendix IV and Fig. 3.10 [p.36]). Although an exercise test should be carried out first, there is a powerful argument for performing coronary angiography in all women below the age of 60 years before a secure diagnosis of angina is made. This should be combined with stress imaging before revascularization is attempted, if the relationship between the coronary disease and symptoms is uncertain. As previously discussed, stress imaging techniques may supplant the need for coronary arteriography but only after confirmation of accuracy by internal audit.

Patients with previous evidence of coronary disease

Many patients with angina will have had a previous MI and some patients will have had a coronary angiogram showing coronary artery disease (see Appendix III). In these patients, there is no doubt that coronary disease is present. A coronary angiogram adds no further diagnostic information in these cases.

Even atypical symptoms should be regarded as angina unless otherwise proven, although patients with coronary disease are also prone to dyspeptic symptoms because of the widespread use of aspirin. In patients with persisting atypical symptoms, despite appropriate antianginal therapy, trials of nitrates versus alginates, H_2 antagonists or proton pump inhibitors, either singly or in combination, are a reasonable therapeutic path. Dyspepsia requiring more than 2 weeks of treatment of frequent recurrent courses of therapy should prompt investigation of the upper gastrointestinal tract. If determining the origin of the patient's symptoms is still difficult despite a therapeutic trial, the patient should have an exercise test, ideally combined with stress imaging, and an endoscopy or barium meal.

Prognosis

After the patient has been diagnosed as having angina, an estimate of prognosis should be made. A clinical history gives most of the information required to determine prognosis, which tends to be much worse in older patients. A nomogram has been developed to relate the results of exercise testing to prognosis and is shown in Figure 4.5 [p. 50].

Major ventricular dysfunction is highly unusual in patients with a normal ECG [9,10]. Echocardiography should be performed in all patients with angina if they have symptoms or signs suggestive of previous MI, major left ventricular dysfunction at rest or a clearly abnormal ECG strong evidence indicates that patients with major impairment (ejection fraction < 40%) of left ventricular function will benefit prognostically from use of ACE inhibitors and probably beta blockers and an argument can be made for surgery in selected individuals even if symptoms are not commanding.

If a patient with severe left ventricular dysfunction (ejection fraction < 30%) is considered a candidate for surgery, then, in view of the higher surgical mortality and morbidity, further investigation is warranted before angiography. Patients should undergo tests to determine the extent of nonfunctioning but viable myocardium that might benefit from surgery because revascularizing irreversible left ventricular damage is unlikely to be of benefit. In those with extensive reversible ischaemia or clear evidence of extensive 'hibernating' myocardium and who are otherwise candidates for revascularization, angiography should be performed.

Clear recommendations for the more widespread use of stress imaging must await appropriate clinical trial data, although, if the service is readily available and of high quality then it can help to select those who will benefit most from coronary intervention [11].

There is no evidence to suggest that angiography is superior to a combination of clinical history, exercise testing and imaging of left ventricular function in identifying those patients who require surgery. Angiography should only be performed when diagnostic doubt persists or when a decision that the patient requires revascularization has already been taken. The reasons for angiography should be stated before catheterization to prevent cosmetic revascularization of patients undergoing diagnostic angiography. Left main coronary disease is unusual in those without a positive exercise test at low level or marked impairment of ventricular function. In patients with left main coronary disease without the above features, the prognosis is favourable and the benefits of surgery uncertain [12,13].

Treatment

Patients with chronic recurrent chest pain can be split into four groups, each needing different management strategies (Fig. 6.3). Psychological support, risk factor management and encouragement to discuss specific problems important to the patient (e.g. sexual relationships, driving, work) probably have at least as great an impact on the quality of the patient's life as do medical therapy or surgery.

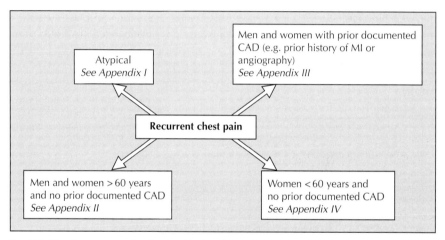

Fig. 6.3. *The four groups of patients with chronic recurrent chest pain.*

Coronary disease

Patients with coronary disease should not smoke and should diet to achieve their ideal weight. Moderate physical activity should be encouraged, mostly for its psychological benefit; little evidence suggests that it alters the coronary event rate.

All patients with coronary disease and a cholesterol level above 5.4 mmol/l should have their lipid levels lowered [14]. For most patients, this means drug therapy: a trial of diet should be continued for no longer than 6 months before drug therapy is started. An alternative, more aggressive approach, is to start diet and drug therapy at once, withdrawing drug therapy if the cholesterol level falls below 5 mmol/l. No evidence indicates that tailoring the type of drug therapy to the lipid profile makes any difference to patient outcome. Although epidemiological studies suggest an important role for triglycerides in coronary disease, such measurements have not been the target of therapy in any of the large intervention trials. Treatment directed primarily at lowering cholesterol is appropriate, given the current state of knowledge.

The clearest evidence of benefit from lipid lowering in angina is with statin therapy. Although treatment with simvastatin may be considered to be at the limit of what is cost-effective for patients with angina [8], the cost of these drugs will hopefully fall with time. Whether statins are superior to fibrates for secondary prevention is unclear. Fibrates are much less expensive than statins and could be considered as an alternative therapy, although they are generally less effective in reducing cholesterol.

Further studies will determine whether all patients with coronary disease, regardless of their blood cholesterol, should have their cholesterol lowered [15,16]. Although the benefits of lipid-lowering therapy have not been established in those over 75 years of age, it seems appropriate to treat these high-risk patients in view of the safety of lipid-lowering therapy.

Routine prescription of aspirin is currently fashionable. Much evidence indicates its benefit in patients with recent MI or unstable angina and therapy should be given for at least 12 weeks. Aspirin is probably of benefit in low-risk patients with stable angina and well preserved ventricular function but may be deleterious in those with heart failure [17]. Combined analysis of all the long-term postinfarction trials failed to show any prognostic benefit with aspirin [17] or any modification of the underlying atherosclerotic process [18].

Angina

The simplest therapy for patients with rare attacks of angina is sublingual nitrates alone or nitrate spray, which has a longer shelf life. For patients with more frequent angina, prophylactic therapy reduces frequency and improves functional capacity. The currently available agents have similar antianginal efficacy (Fig. 6.4).

Patient group	Drug of choice	Other options	Avoid
Angina only	Beta blockers, calcium antagonists or nitrates alone, or beta blocker + calcium antagonist in combination		
Asthma, COAD	Calcium antagonists, nitrates		Beta blockers
Heart failure	Nitrates	Calcium antagonists, beta blockers, long-acting dihydropyridine (e.g. nifedipine GITS, amlodipine)	Short-acting calcium antagonist
Diabetes	Calcium antagonists, nitrates	Beta blockers	
Peripheral vascular disease	Calcium antagonists, nitrates	Beta blockers	

Fig. 6.4. *Treatment of angina with other diseases. COAD, chronic obstructive airway disease; GITS, gastrointestinal therapeutic system.*

First generation, standard preparation dihydropyridine calcium antagonists were associated with a high frequency of minor side effects and a worrying increase in coronary events and mortality compared with placebo in several studies [19,20]. In contrast, studies with newer formulations of nifedipine (slow-release or gastrointestinal therapeutic system) have not shown an increase in coronary events [21–23]. Long-acting calcium antagonists have proved to be safe in patients with heart failure and coronary disease and could be used to relieve angina in this population (see Fig. 6.4). Studies that have combined dihydropyridine calcium antagonists with a beta blocker suggest that this combination may have a lower serious event rate than either agent used alone. Whether this reflects greater antianginal efficacy, a greater effect on blood pressure or synergistic effects on the natural history of coronary disease is not clear. Combinations of beta blockers and dihydropyridine calcium antagonists may become standard first-line therapy without contraindications to either component, although the data are not yet conclusive.

Postinfarction studies with diltiazem have not shown any change in the incidence of serious adverse events, whereas studies with verapamil suggest that it may reduce serious events but is contraindicated in patients with heart failure [24].

Beta blockers have been shown to reduce mortality and reinfarction after an initial infarction [24] but they failed to reduce mortality in elderly patients with hypertension [25]. No evidence suggests that they alter mortality in patients with angina. Beta blockers should be avoided in those with asthma or a major reversible element to chronic obstructive airway disease. They should also be used with caution in patients with heart failure, although, when initiated in low doses and increased slowly, they have proved to be remarkably safe and may reduce worsening of heart failure [8]. Relative contraindications include insulin-dependent diabetes. The frequency of minor side effects with beta blockers is high.

Nitrates have few serious side effects but must be used intelligently to avoid tolerance. No evidence suggests that nitrates affect the natural history of coronary disease or reduce mortality after MI [24]. However, some evidence indicates that nitrates may improve symptoms of heart failure and possibly modify outcome [26,27]. Nicorandil may be considered a nitrate for practical purposes and has not been shown to alter outcome in angina.

Revascularization should be performed in patients with intractable symptoms despite treatment with adequate doses of at least two antianginal agents and in those who are unable to tolerate medical therapy. Revascularization to improve prognosis should be considered under the following conditions:

- A strongly positive exercise text suggesting an annual mortality > 4%. The predicted risk of MI should not be included because no evidence suggests that surgery or PTCA revascularization reduces the overall risk of infarction, even in unstable angina.

- Major resting left ventricular dysfunction and a large reversible component on stress imaging, although adequate trials on the clinical use of revascularizing hibernating myocardium are awaited.

Management of unstable angina

The diagnosis of unstable angina can be at least as difficult as that of stable angina. A low initial diagnostic threshold for unstable angina is appropriate while excluding alternative causes for pain (Fig. 6.5). A classification of unstable angina as suggested by Braunwald [28] (see Fig. 5.20 [p. 86]) is a useful concept to help identify groups who require special treatment (e.g. unstable angina precipitated by gastrointestinal haemorrhage or rapid atrial fibrillation) and groups with varying prognosis (new-onset exertional angina versus persistent rest angina).

System	Diagnosis
Cardiopulmonary	MI Pericarditis (pneumonia) Pulmonary embolus Pneumothorax Aortic dissection
Gastrointestinal	Reflux oesophagitis Peptic ulcer Oesophageal rupture Cholecystitis
Chest wall	Various poorly defined entities

Fig. 6.5. *Differential diagnosis of unstable angina.*

Unstable angina can be classified into:

• New onset (manage as for stable angina but accelerate the diagnostic process)

• Worsening exertional angina (manage as for stable angina but accelerate the diagnostic process)

• Angina worsening and occurring at rest

A patient with unstable angina at rest should be referred to hospital, preferably a coronary care unit and certainly a place where serial ECGs can be done during and after resolution of pain.

Aspirin should be given prophylactically while awaiting a firm diagnosis and further treatment should be withheld until the diagnosis has been confirmed, usually by typical ECG changes and their reversal with nitrate therapy. The treatment strategy for a patient with suspected unstable angina is shown in Figure 6.6. ECG leads should be recorded to the right of the sternum and from posterior chest leads in patients with suspicious symptoms but no ECG changes. Treatment before confirming the diagnosis clouds the clinical picture and may delay definitive treatment and discharge. When diagnostic doubt persists, an angiogram should be performed early. In reality, many patients are managed in hospitals without

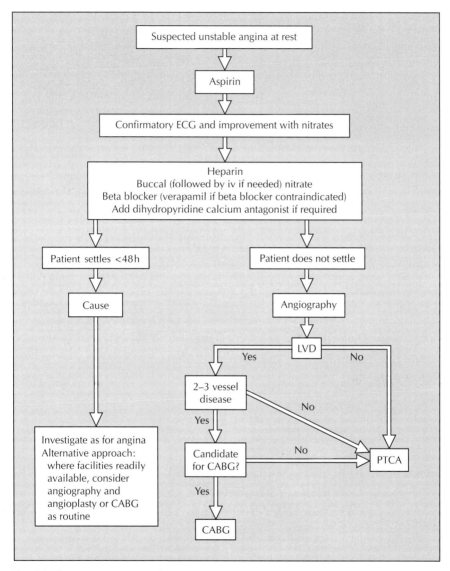

Fig. 6.6 *The treatment strategy for a patient with suspected unstable angina. LVD, left ventricular dysfunction.*

angiographic facilities and in such cases full treatment may be instituted without a complete diagnosis.

After the diagnosis is determined, the patient should receive heparin and a beta blocker in addition to intravenous or buccal nitrates. In severe cases, an intravenous

109

beta blocker such as esmolol may be given. In patients with respiratory contraindications to beta blockers, verapamil should be given. The target heart rate is 50–60 beats/min. If bradycardia is present before therapy or there is a markedly prolonged P-R interval or 2:1 atrioventricular block, the patient should have diltiazem or a long-acting preparation of a dihydropyridine calcium antagonist rather than a beta blocker or verapamil. The addition of dihydropyridine calcium antagonists to a beta blocker is safe and often effective.

If the pain does not settle within 48 h, the patient should be referred for angiography with a view to angioplasty or CABG. Patients with severe unstable angina should be investigated by coronary angiography at a much earlier stage. For patients with refractory unstable angina, in whom a definitive procedure cannot be performed immediately, intra-aortic balloon pumping can be remarkably effective. Such procedures can now be performed with little difficulty in the coronary care unit using percutaneous systems and should be used on a more widespread basis. If no definitive coronary procedure is feasible, then balloon pumping could be used, although this should be used with caution because weaning the patient off it may be difficult.

Patients whose pain settles should be assessed in the same way as patients with chronic angina. In those whose pain settles, heparin should be discontinued after 3–5 days.

An alternative approach is to perform early angiography with PTCA or CABG on all patients. No evidence indicates that this reduces the rate of death or infarction but it does lower the risk of recurrent hospitalization and total days spent in hospital. This may have important implications in terms not only of patient preference, but also of cost.

References

1. Lichtlen PR et al.: Anatomical progression of coronary artery disease in humans as seen by prospective, repeated, quantified coronary angiography. Relation to clinical events and risk factors. The INTACT Study Group. Circulation 1992, 86:828–838.
2. Bruschke AV et al.: The natural history of angiographically demonstrated coronary heart disease. Eur Heart J 1992, 13:70–75.
3. Hackett D et al.: Pre-existing coronary stenoses in patients with first myocardial infarction are not necessarily severe. Eur Heart J 1988, 9:1317–1323.
4. Little WC et al.: Can coronary angiography predict the site of a subsequent myocardial infarction in patients with mild-to-moderate coronary artery disease? Circulation 1988, 78:1157–1166.
5. Yusuf S et al.: Effect of coronary artery bypass graft surgery on survival: overview of 10-year results from randomised trials by the Coronary Artery Bypass Graft Surgery Trialists Collaboration. Lancet 1994, 344:563–570.
6. Hartz AJ et al.: Mortality after coronary angioplasty and coronary artery bypass surgery (The National Medicare Experience). Am J Cardiol 1992, 70:179–185.
7. Roper WL et al.: Effectiveness in health care. An initiative to evaluate and improve medical practice. N Eng J Med 1988, 319:1197–1202.
8. Cleland JGF: Beta-blocking agents in heart failure. Should they be used and how? Eur Heart J 1995, in press.
9. Rihal CS et al.: The utility of clinical, electro-cardiographic, and roentgenographic variables in the prediction of left ventricular function. Am J Cardiol 1995, 75:220–223.
10. Francis CM et al.: Open access echocardiography in management of heart failure in the community. BMJ 1995, 310:634–636.
11. Ladenheim ML et al.: Extent and severity of myocardial hypoperfusion as predictors of prognosis in patients with suspected coronary artery disease. J Am Coll Cardiol 1986, 7:464–471.
12. Taylor HA et al.: Asymptomatic left main coronary artery disease in the Coronary Artery Surgery Study (CASS) registry. Circulation 1989 79:1171–1179.
13. Hueb W et al.: Two- to eight-year survival rates in patients who refused coronary artery bypass grafting. Am J Cardiol 1989, 63:155–159.
14. Pedersen TR: Randomised trial of cholesterol lowering in 4444 patients with coronary heart

in patients who refused coronary artery bypass grafting. *Am J Cardiol* 1989, **63**:155–159.

14. Pedersen TR: **Randomised trial of cholesterol lowering in 4444 patients with coronary heart disease: the Scandinavian Simvastatin Survival Study (4S).** *Lancet* 1994, **344**:1383–1389.

15. Sacks FM: **Is there anything to add to our lipid risk factors for coronary heart disease? [Editorial].** *Am J Cardiol* 1995, **75**:1623–1264.

16. Simes RJ: **Prospective meta-analysis of cholesterol-lowering studies. The Prospective Pravastatin Lowering Project and the Cholesterol Treatment trialists Collaboration.** *Am J Cardiol* 1995, **76**:122C–126C.

17. Cleland JGF *et al.*: **Is aspirin safe for patients with heart failure?** *Br Heart J* 1995, **74**:215–217.

18. Cleland JGF, Krikler DM: **Modification of atherosclerosis by agents that do not lower cholesterol.** *Br Heart J* 1993, **69(suppl)**:554–562.

19. Held PH *et al.*: **Calcium channel blockers in acute myocardial infarction and unstable angina: an overview.** *BMJ* 1989, **299**:1187–1192.

20. Furberg CD *et al.*: **Nifedipine: dose-related increase in mortality in patients with coronary heart disease.** *Circulation* 1995, **92**:1326–1331.

21. Opie H *et al.*: **Nifedipine and mortality: grave defects in the dossier.** *Circulation* 1995, **92**:1068–1073.

22. Kloner RA: **Nifedipine in ischemic heart disease.** *Circulation* 1995, **92**:1074–1078.

23. Gonser M *et al.*: **Meta-analyses of interventional trials done in populations with different risks [Letter].** *Lancet* 1995, **345**:1304.

24. Cleland J, McMurray J, Ray S (eds): *Prevention Strategies After Myocardial Infarction*. London: Science Press; 1994.

25. Lever AF, Brennan PJ: **MRC trial of treatment in elderly hypertensives.** *Clin Exp Hypertens* 1993, **15**:941–952.

26. Cohn JN *et al.*: **Effect of vasodilator therapy on mortality in chronic congestive heart failure. Results of a Veterans Administration Cooperative Study.** *N Eng J Med* 1986, **314**:1547–1552.

27. Loeb HS *et al.*: **Effect of enalapril, hydralazine plus isosorbide dinitrate, and prazosin on hospitalization in patients with chronic congestive heart failure. The V-HeFT VA Cooperative Studies Group.** *Circulation* 1993, **87(suppl)**:V178–V187.

28. Braunwald E *et al.*: **Diagnosing and managing unstable angina.** *Circulation* 1994, **90**:613–622.

Appendix I

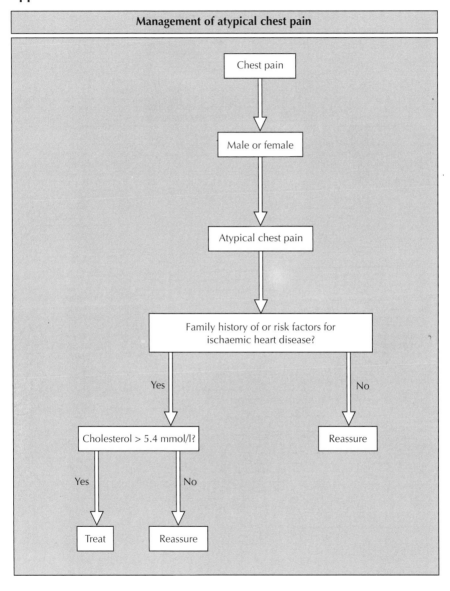

Management of atypical chest pain

Chest pain

Male or female

Atypical chest pain

Family history of or risk factors for ischaemic heart disease?

Yes | No

Cholesterol > 5.4 mmol/l? | Reassure

Yes | No

Treat | Reassure

Appendix II

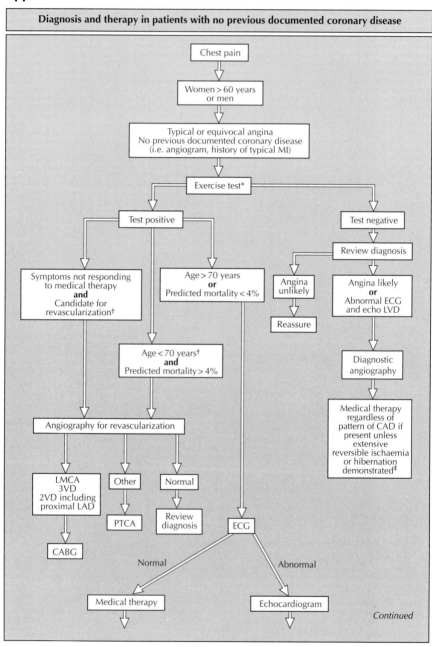

Diagnosis and therapy in patients with no previous documented coronary disease

Continued

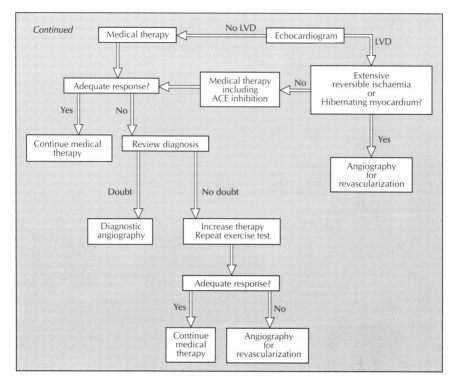

Angiography is divided into angiography for revascularization and diagnostic angiography. The latter should not lead to revascularization without the demonstration of extensive reversible myocardial ischaemia. CAD, coronary artery disease; LVD, left ventricular dysfunction; LAD, left anterior descending VD, vessel disease.

*On therapy if principal aim is to assess prognosis, off therapy if principal aim is to assess diagnosis. Mainly to assess prognosis in men with typical angina and for diagnosis and prognosis in all women and in men with equivocal symptoms.

† An age limit of less than 65 years for women may be appropriate because the operative mortality for women is considerably higher than for men. The biological age of the patient should lead to some flexibility around chronological age cut-off point. The higher threshold for revascularization for prognosis in older age groups reflects the higher operative mortality. Failure of medical therapy is an indication for revascularization regardless of age or sex with very few exceptions.

‡ The relative sensitivity and specificity of echocardiographic and radionuclide tests for assessing myocardial viability are still disputed. The evidence that any of these methods can predict clinical outcome, rather than recovery of wall motion, in patients with very poor ventricular function is preliminary and although encouraging, is not conclusive.

Appendix III

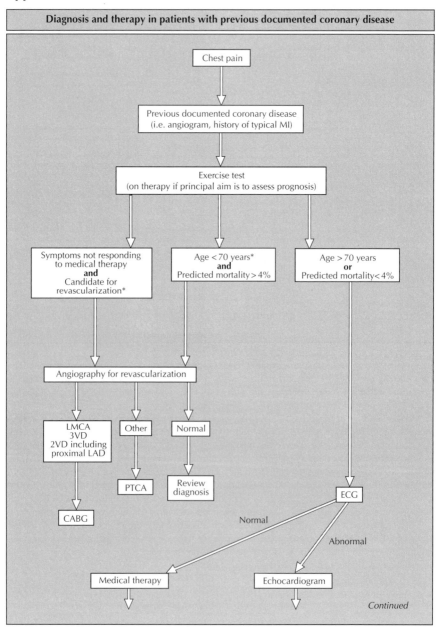

Diagnosis and therapy in patients with previous documented coronary disease

Chest pain

Previous documented coronary disease
(i.e. angiogram, history of typical MI)

Exercise test
(on therapy if principal aim is to assess prognosis)

Symptoms not responding
to medical therapy
and
Candidate for
revascularization*

Age <70 years*
and
Predicted mortality > 4%

Age > 70 years
or
Predicted mortality< 4%

Angiography for revascularization

LMCA
3VD
2VD including
proximal LAD

Other

Normal

PTCA

Review
diagnosis

ECG

CABG

Normal

Abnormal

Medical therapy

Echocardiogram

Continued

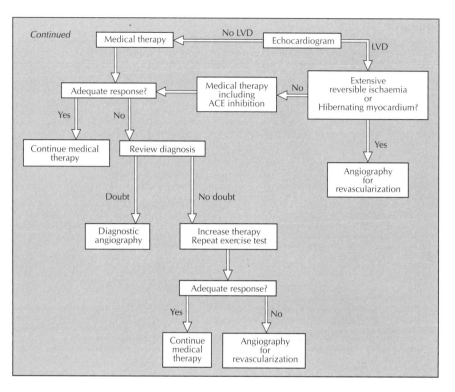

Angiography is divided into angiography for revascularization and diagnostic angiography. The latter should not lead to revascularization without the demonstration of extensive reversible myocardial ischaemia. LVD, left ventricular dysfunction; LAD, left anterior descending; LMCA, left main coronary artery; VD, vessel disease.

*An age limit of less than 65 years for women may be appropriate as the operative mortality for women is considerably higher than for men. The biological age of the patient should lead to some flexibility around chronological age cut-off point. The higher threshold for revascularization for prognosis in older age groups reflects the higher operative mortality. Failure of medical therapy is an indication for revascularization regardless of age or gender with very few exceptions.

Appendix IV

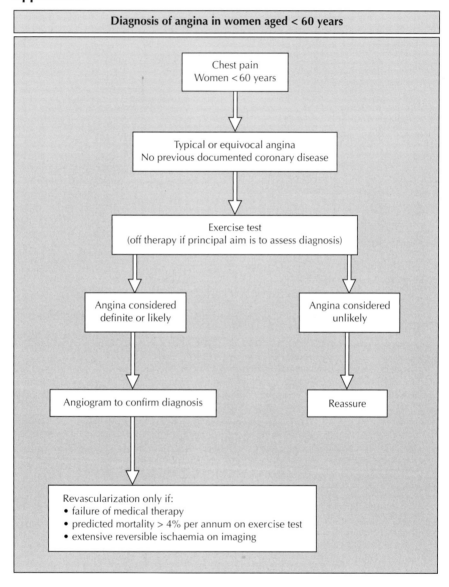

Diagnosis of angina in women aged < 60 years

Chest pain
Women < 60 years

Typical or equivocal angina
No previous documented coronary disease

Exercise test
(off therapy if principal aim is to assess diagnosis)

Angina considered
definite or likely

Angina considered
unlikely

Angiogram to confirm diagnosis

Reassure

Revascularization only if:
• failure of medical therapy
• predicted mortality > 4% per annum on exercise test
• extensive reversible ischaemia on imaging

Index

119